FROM IGNORED
TO ADORED

Published by Grammar Factory Publishing, an imprint of MacMillan Company Limited.

Grammar Factory Publishing
MacMillan Company Limited
25 Telegram Mews, 39th Floor, Suite 3906
Toronto, Ontario, Canada
M5V 3Z1

www.grammarfactory.com

Taylor, Shani.
From Ignored to Adored: Ignite Connection and Communication Online to Attract Your Soul Mate Clients...Without Being Salesy

Paperback ISBN 978-1-998756-1-31
Hardcover ISBN 978-1-998756-1-55
eBook ISBN 978-1-998756-1-48

1. BUS025000 BUSINESS & ECONOMICS / Entrepreneurship. 2. BUS058000 BUSINESS & ECONOMICS / Sales & Selling / General. 3. BUS090010 BUSINESS & ECONOMICS / E-Commerce / Digital Marketing.

Production Credits
Cover design by Designerbility
Interior layout design by Dania Zafar
Book production and editorial services by Grammar Factory Publishing

Grammar Factory's Carbon Neutral Publishing Commitment
Grammar Factory Publishing is proud to be neutralising the carbon footprint of all printed copies of its authors' books printed by or ordered directly through Grammar Factory or its affiliated companies through the purchase of Gold Standard-Certified International Offsets.

FROM IGNORED TO ADORED

Ignite Connection and Communication Online to Attract Your Soul Mate Clients...Without Being Salesy

SHANI TAYLOR

Thank you to my past, present and future clients for allowing me to serve you. You have helped create the content that finds its home in these pages.

TESTIMONIALS

Helping people make a buying decision. Put very simply, this is what this book does. But more than that, Shani Taylor pulls apart how we connect. Not communicate. It's deeper than that. It's about connecting. We can read all the books on sales. Rewatch *Mad Men* episodes. Take NLP training to try and 'hack' our ability to persuade others. Or we can learn how to improve our ability to connect. Human to human. And maybe, this book will help you improve all of your relationships like it has done for me.

– JO MUIRHEAD, HEALTH PROFESSIONAL AND COACH

If you're someone who lives a heart-centred life and you're passionate about serving clients, Shani Taylor's playbook delivers a concise method for communicating with and connecting to prospective clients. You want to truly connect with potential clients rather than stalking them like an online bot? There are strategies in these pages to teach you how to connect. You want to discover why your social media strategies aren't working? There are insights here. Want to move from discouraged to inspired? Yes, there's help here. This book is a great resource for discovering how to generate clients in a sincere, effective way by communicating in a way that is meaningful to potential clients and drawing them towards you rather than having them running away.

– ASH PERROW, MUSICIAN AND CREATIVE FREEDOM COACH

If you're looking to grow your business using proven methods, so you can experience more freedom and fulfilment in your life, Shani Taylor's *From Ignored to Adored* is the book for you. *From Ignored to Adored* is a practical and actionable guide to growing your business using frameworks and methods that work. It also teaches readers how to connect and build relationships with their audience. It includes real-life examples of client success using these principles and methods. Shani's sense of humour is sprinkled throughout the book, making for an enjoyable read. In this book, you will learn how to consistently attract the clients that you feel inspired to serve, and how to build relationships with them so they don't want to leave. You will learn how to connect with your audience in all your communications in a way that attracts instead of repels them. Your audience will feel like you are talking directly to them and will want to do business with you and not the competition.

The coaching industry is the second largest-growing sector in the world, with approximately 5,842,000 coaches worldwide. Most coaching schools teach the skills to become a coach but don't teach how to build a successful business. There are business and marketing coaches who offer programs to launch and grow your coaching business, but the problem is they use methods that are outdated and do not deliver on their promises. Coaches eventually get tired, frustrated, and quit, unable to share their gifts with the world. *From Ignored to Adored* is a beam of light in an industry clouded with old ideas that no longer work and that continue to get regurgitated from mentors to coaches.

– ANA RUIZ, RELATIONSHIP COACH

This book is a masterpiece. It's a reset and redirect of my mindset towards truth and reality. I feel more relieved doing more of my business and rejecting inquiries from people I don't feel inspired to serve. For me, it's a bible for resetting my business and I feel sorry about all the time I wasted hearing the lies I've been told by people whom I trusted. The book deserves a re-read many times, and it's a must for anyone who is doing business today. It has a lot of truth, and it is like someone has turned the light on in all areas of my life.

– ANEES ALOMAR, ARCHITECT AND BUSINESS CONSULTANT

This book is a must read for anyone wanting to understand the true art of human connection and modern-day marketing success! Shani's no-nonsense style is delivered with integrity and authenticity, from a deep place of understanding! It's a very clever recipe of how to connect with and build audiences online – in a deeper, more meaningful way – than I have ever learned from the many coaches I have worked with! An invaluable read for building an online business, while also helping you with your own deeper connections to family, friends and colleagues in everyday life.

– SUE KOHN-TAYLOR, PEOPLE DEVELOPMENT AND MENTAL FITNESS EXPERT

CONTENTS

Introduction

Introduction

I felt like I'd been fighting all my life.

Fighting to be seen and heard. Fighting to be cared for or cared about.

Fighting to connect.

My life was created as the by-product of an affair. My father is a Sicilian immigrant and was married and already had a family when he employed my mother as a salesperson at his car yard in the early 1980s. My mother was simply a fling for him, but she thought she was in love. And like many 'other women' who have affairs with married men, she thought one day my father would leave his wife. He didn't, and the story goes that when my mother shared the news that she was expecting, he told her to abort the pregnancy or he'd blow her kneecaps off. Clearly, she didn't abort her pregnancy and her kneecaps are still intact, but I grew up without a biological father in my life. Nor did he provide any financial support. My mother did her best and, even though she was physically present, she was often mentally and emotionally absent. She had issues of her own that she was dealing with caused by her traumatic childhood.

At the age of sixteen I was out of home and picked up an intravenous drug addiction. I fought that addiction off, but as any addict will tell you, it wasn't easy. I could have become a statistic, still using, or worse, dead.

At twenty-three, due to a relationship breakdown, I effectively became a single mum when my son was just eleven weeks old. Again, I was fighting. I fought for our time together, for our safety and security, and for our future.

The fight for life and survival had become so strong within me I didn't know any other way of being, and what's worse is I didn't even realise I was always in fight mode. I was constantly at war with something or someone – often myself.

The fight had its benefits. Being out of home at a young age and in the company of other drug addicts, you quickly learn how to survive; how to read people, and how to respond to the tension that often happens when people are on drugs by helping them to simmer down. The fight also taught me to value my communication skills and grow them, so I could go on to build a career and have the financial resources to ensure my son and I didn't have to live in poverty. Knowing how to connect and communicate are imperative if you want to start and grow a business or have impact in this world and live a fulfilled life.

But the fight hadn't ended.

In 2011, I was held under duress in a house for two days and repeatedly sexually assaulted by a family member. They told me that if I escaped they'd find me and kill me and my son.

I did escape – physically – but I spent many years afterwards feeling mentally and emotionally chained to that experience.

I was worried that person would come kill us.

So, I changed my last name in an attempt to stop them from finding me. I had all my social media profiles locked down to private and random profile pictures that weren't me, so that there were no iden-tifying details. After the event, this person was so obsessed they had even started a fake Facebook account pretending to be me.

Being online didn't feel safe. Neither did being in 'real life'.

I was scared.

I was hiding.

It was no way to live – enough was enough.

I invested time, money and energy on working through the dark-ness until I got to the light. I realised that I had been letting that experience, and all the fighting I had done in the past, stop me from living in the present.

Through doing the inner work, I saw that even in that experience of horror, I had been left with some incredible gifts and it was up to me to make the most of them. One of those gifts was a deepened awareness of how to read humans and communicate in a connected way in any situation; to be proactive rather than reactive.

During the two days that I was held under duress, I was constantly on alert and had to read my captor's behaviour to effectively communicate with them and create as much 'calmness' in the situation as possible. The situation was volatile, and I didn't want it to escalate to the point where I was in danger of being killed.

If you don't know how to communicate with others at every level, in any situation, in a way they can hear you, your life is a constant battle. Communication is what connects and brings people together – or separates us.

The skill of reading human behaviour and communicating in a connected way is now what I teach people to do so they can grow their businesses authentically and share their unique gifts with the world. Being in business, you will experience conflict almost every day. Those who survive and thrive in business are the people who can remain stable in response to the disruption of other people's words and emotions. Who can lead the connection and conversation in a way that is fulfilling for everyone.

People often say that the skills they learn from me flow into other areas of their lives, and they feel more connected to themselves and their loved ones. This lights me up.

I probably wouldn't be where I am today without all the experiences I've shared with you here, and the lessons they taught me.

That event in 2011 was the catalyst for deep change and what led me to create my own business. Before that, I had been existing aimlessly, with little clarity on what I wanted to do with my life. I was living every day feeling deeply unfulfilled. I had been simply fighting for survival. Now, I know how I want to impact the world and I get to spend my days doing just that.

Being connected to a fulfilling purpose and living every day from that space within you creates a life worth living. It took courage to start my online business because I was worried that, by opening up a public profile, I'd open myself up to be hurt again.

It's taken even more courage to keep growing, to become MORE visible and be SEEN by more people.

I started my business with no audience, no network, and no idea how to find clients or create content that connects and sells to them. But through taking action and learning every day, I quickly worked out what didn't work and what did. As a result, my business made a quarter of a million dollars in its first year and has continued to grow every year since.

How did I go from being scared and hiding to being open, public and sharing this story with you today?

It was the realisation that to do anything other than share my gifts and fulfil my potential would have been to waste the precious life I had left.

Maybe you can relate?

Maybe there's something inside you longing to come out, but you're still playing it small and safe? You're still not living up to what you know, deep down, you're truly capable of, because you had an experience that taught you that the world wasn't safe. That it wasn't safe to be yourself.

You've dimmed your light because of it.

When you do that, it's not only you who misses out. It's all the people you can inspire and impact that miss out, too. When your past is still running your present, you're playing small. What's still left inside you that is aching to be expressed? Don't let your fear win. It is never too late to make a change in your life. You are never too old to become more of yourself. It is safe to be you.

It's time to play bigger. It's time to learn how to better connect and communicate with the people you'd love to serve. The people who are waiting for you to show up and help them transform their lives.

Your time is always now.

The world is waiting for you.

....

If you don't know how to communicate with others at every level, in any situation, in a way they can hear you, your life is a constant battle.

....

PART 1

CLARITY

CHAPTER 1:

The curse you were born with

Walt Disney, founder of The Walt Disney Company and creator of many of the movies we loved to watch as kids – movies like *Mary Poppins*, *Pinocchio* and *Snow White and the Seven Dwarfs* – had a vision when he set out to share his gift with the world. He wanted to bring families together through experiences and content, and I think you'd agree that he achieved his goal. What you may not realise, however, is that he has also done the opposite in that he has kept some families *apart* and *disconnected*. It seems outrageous, I know, but hear me out. You might even agree once we walk this path together.

Disney movies are based on fairy tales and fantasies that have created and continue to create unrealistic expectations in the minds of viewers. Expectations that can't be achieved in real life, no matter how hard you try. For example, many young girls and boys watch these fairy tales and form a picture of what love and relationships should look like. When they grow up, they search for the 'knight in shining armour' who will save them or the subservient princess who admires and adores them. When these children reach adulthood, whether they're conscious to it or not, they have an unrealistic expectation of what they will find in a partner and relationship. They continue to feel disappointed and disconnected with each 'failed' relationship, but no one can live up to a fantasy that was birthed from a movie. Maybe you can relate?

....

That's the problem with fantasies – they turn into your nightmares when you keep trying – and failing – to make them real.

....

Similar to the romantic fairy tale you were sold as a kid, you've also been sold a fairy tale about how much better life will be once you start your own business. You've seen the gurus like Tony Robbins and Oprah do it, and from the outside it looks like they're living incredible lives. Admired by the masses, highly influential, travelling the world and enjoying financial success – they've got everything they could ever want. You want that, too. To be loved and appreciated for your gifts, to be able to buy whatever you want, to have the freedom and flexibility to work when you want, where you want.

Seems perfect, right? Wrong.

The influential gurus might look like they've got it all, and they might make it look easy, but what you don't see is that their so-called overnight success took a long time to create. You don't see the eighteen-hour days they poured into their mission to get them to where they are today, or the long hours they still sometimes work because that's what it takes to create, maintain and serve as a highly influential and successful person in business and in the world.

Have you ever wondered why so few people reach that level of influence and true financial freedom? It's because few people are prepared to do what it takes, consistently and every day, to get there. It's not easy to live and breathe your business day in, day out, for years, but that's what it takes to grow and become a Tony Robbins or Oprah. Then, once you've built your business empire and it's flowing with success, you actually have more responsibility, which requires more time and attention from you. The bigger your mission and business, the more people you're responsible for and the more time and energy you have to give. That is the difference between creating a job for yourself and creating a business that is the vehicle for your lifelong mission and that allows you to serve humanity.

This unrealistic expectation of life being easy once you have a business is partly what leads to disappointment and frustration for many who go into business. It's no wonder that, statistically, most businesses close down within the first five years of operation. Many people go into business because they want time and financial freedom. They think they'll be able to work less and sit on a beach sipping cocktails, but the reality is that to begin with you'll find yourself working more. Maybe you're experiencing a taste of this nightmare right now. You thought starting your business would be your ticket to freedom, but it's left you feeling more chained than your nine-to-five did.

It looked easy to start an online business, didn't it? Those damn gurus sold you the dream (a.k.a. the fantasy!). Create an 'irresistible offer', produce some content, share online and voila! All your wildest dreams of sticking it to the man would become a reality and you'd gallop off into the sunset and live happily ever after. But that hasn't happened. What the fantasy-maker (guru) didn't tell you is that you'd end up spending thousands of dollars on yourself in mentorship and coaching programs, only to be told the same thing over and over again about how to grow your business until eventually you wear yourself out, burn out, and still don't have the results you want.

Just like the Disney movies, the gurus and those coaching programs you've invested in stop the story before it's finished. You were sold a fantasy, not the reality – you were swept up in a whirlwind romance and quickly said 'I do', but now it's time to find out how to make the marriage work or, in this case, how to make your business work.

....

So how do you make your business work so you can create freedom and flexibility, rather than live a fantasy-turned-nightmare?

....

TIME FOR A REALITY CHECK

You got started in business so you could share your message and mission with the world and touch people's lives, and because you wanted to create financial and lifestyle freedom for yourself. To be able to work anywhere in the world, at any time that suits you, is what dreams are made of. But the reality is that the pursuit of building your impact and influence, and creating freedom for yourself, has now turned into a heavy burden that is weighing you down.

Right now, you're questioning yourself. The energy and enthusiasm you once had for your business has been drained from your heart and body, and now your soul is tired.

You're not frustrated because you don't want to share your message or impact lives anymore. You're frustrated because the work you need to do to achieve those goals is exhausting.

At the time of writing, there are an estimated 5,842,000 entrepreneurs in the world, and most of them are swinging between feast or famine with very little consistency in revenue or growth. Like you, they can't figure out why things aren't working for them. Like you, they're getting on social media to attract clients and following the methods everyone else is. So, why isn't it working?

It's because you've been sold a lie.

You've been told to:

- ❏ Create an 'I-help' statement
- ❏ Create a Facebook business page
- ❏ Show up on social media every day
- ❏ Share content multiple times a day
- ❏ Share the 'hard knocks' story of what you've achieved in your life and business
- ❏ Add 100 new friends a week
- ❏ Send cold direct messages to those new friends
- ❏ Post pictures of your food, your dog, your kids
- ❏ Share inspirational quotes
- ❏ Make direct offers
- ❏ Go live

- ❑ Run free challenges
- ❑ Give away freebies...

Now read that list again and check off the ones you have tried or are currently doing. Has doing those things brought you clients? Consistently? If it had, wouldn't you be further along in your business by now? And not exhausted?

The list is endless and confusing. Every time you decide to put in the effort to show up on social media, to do lead generation activities and to share content, you get caught up in wondering, 'Is this the right place to start and the right thing to share?'

....

Growing your business, creating content and doing lead generation activities has become a chore rather than an opportunity for you to connect with people and serve them.

....

Worst of all is that you've tried it all and it's not converting to consistent clients. In fact, it's barely converting to likes and you're left wondering why.

So, you do more in the hope that you'll get a result. You create more content, do more sharing, comment more on other people's content and add more friends, because this is what all those business coaches told you to do. You see everyone else doing it, so it must be working, right? Wrong. All you're doing is adding to the online noise – which is being ignored – and making yourself anxious because your time would be better spent elsewhere. But you're desperate for more clients, and you want to find people to serve online because that's what you were told you have to do.

Here's the truth.

....

It's not the WHAT you're doing that is so much the problem. It's HOW you're doing it.

....

IT'S WHAT, NOT HOW; AND WITH, NOT AT

The average person scrolls the entire length of the Statue of Liberty every single day! When you add this to the fact that the average social media user currently has an attention span of 1.8 seconds, you begin to understand how difficult it is to stop your audience in their scroll and keep their attention on your content.

Think about this. How often do you stop in your scroll and not only stop, but consume someone's entire piece of content? Less than a handful of times a day, right? It's the same for the people you're trying to connect with. Every time you pick up your smartphone you're bombarded with notifications for text messages, missed calls, emails, banking apps and social media. In fact, there are over sixty billion messages sent out across digital platforms every single day. It's no wonder you and your audience are overwhelmed and overstimulated.

Yes, you do have to undertake certain activities – like bringing in new 'friends' who are potential clients and creating conversations with them. And you do have to share content so those potential clients know if your message resonates with them and can decide whether to work with you. But it's HOW you're doing it that is downright terrible and why your efforts are not converting to clients for you. You're not even getting seen by potential clients most of the time, and you don't realise this. You're doing the same things in the same way with the same message as your competitors, who are also on social media vying for the attention of your target audience. You're getting lost in the sea of noise.

....

You have to know how to pierce through all that overwhelming noise so that your people can hear and see you.

....

The constant effort you put into your lead generation activities – like adding new friends and sharing content online – gives you very little engagement or conversion, and it's soul crushing.

And you're right. They don't care about you. No one cares about you unless you can tell them why they should in the way that's most meaningful to them. And what's most meaningful to them is themselves, because just like you, they are I-centric. This is why what you, and every other service provider, is doing online isn't so much the problem as *how* you're doing it. Right now, when you share content, you're speaking AT your audience, rather than being in conversation WITH them. There's a subtle but powerful difference here that can take you from being ignored to being adored.

....

You need to stop speaking AT people and start speaking WITH them.

....

YOUR I-CENTRICITY IS HOLDING YOU BACK

The word 'centric' means 'concentrated about or directed to a centre activity', so when we bring the words 'I' and 'centric' together, we have a word that means you've placed yourself at the centre of your communication and how you connect. The tricky part is that, because you have good intentions, you're blind to how your I-centricity influences the actions you take and the way you communicate. It's your good intentions that prevent you from seeing clearly that what you're doing and how you're communicating is all about you, and is therefore disconnecting you from others.

Let's look at some examples of how you display your I-centricity in your business and on social media:

- ❏ You create content about what YOU want to talk about rather than being informed by what your audience is currently interested in.
- ❏ Your content and communication are filled with sentences that start with 'I' – a quick look at your website, and you'll have a chuckle at yourself right now. Go take a look at your content on social media – full of 'I' sentences too, yes?
- ❏ When someone asks you what you do, you lead with an 'I-help' statement.

❑   In trying to be helpful, you offer advice to people even when they don't ask for it. When you're on social media and you see people talking about things that you know you have insights into, do you write comments telling them what you know in your attempt to be helpful? That's you being I-centric.

You can see now what I meant when I said you have the best of intentions and think you're being helpful in the way you communicate. But these 'good intentions' get in the way of seeing what's really going on. What's really going on is that you're being I-centric and separating yourself from others.

As a human being, you are hardwired to automatically and constantly be thinking about yourself; speaking for yourself, speaking about yourself, and seeking to get what you want and need from any connection and communication with very little consideration for the individuals you are speaking to. This is the nature of being human and we are all the same. You are speaking AT people rather than WITH them – and they are doing the same to you. And it all began the moment you were born.

You may have been adored or ignored as a child; either way it has made you I-centric.

....

Being I-centric means you're communicating for YOU.

....

If you were adored as a baby, you were taught that the world is about you. You only had to cry, wink, gurgle, or make any movement at all, and you were showered with attention. You learned that the world revolves around you. As you moved through your toddler years to your pre-teens, you experienced life through your feelings, and related to others and the world through the lens of how it all affects you. You had very little thought about how others were experiencing life or experiencing YOU. (Hard pill to swallow, I know, but keep reading. It gets better, I promise.)

Then came adolescence, and this stage of life was increasingly challenging as you navigated the hormones surging within you and the emotions they create. At the same time, you attempted to understand the external world and find your place in society as adulthood knocked on your door.

By now your I-centricity is so deeply ingrained that this is your modus operandi, and you're reading this and telling yourself, 'This isn't me.' That voice telling you it isn't you is your I-centricity speaking, and it's what stops you from having more people to serve because it repels potential clients. But you can transform this; don't worry, I've got you.

Maybe you *weren't* adored as a child. Maybe you were ignored.

If you were ignored as a child, you learned that no one cared about you. You went into survival mode and had to make life about you because no one else was doing it. Your I-centricity runs deep because it's driven by your survival instinct, but it's those challenges from childhood that have made you want to serve humanity and change the world. You know from the emptiness you feel inside that it's time to control your I-centricity instead of letting it control you.

By default, your mind is constantly thinking about you – what you want, what you need and what you desire. In fact, when you aren't focused on solving a definitive problem, ninety-five per cent of the time you're thinking about YOURSELF. And so is every other individual on this earth.

So, every single day, we have close to eight billion people roaming the world and speaking AT one another rather than WITH each other. It's no wonder we're at war with ourselves and each other.

....

From the moment you are born and throughout your childhood, you are not taught how to truly connect with others. Now it's showing up in your business, your message and how you communicate.

....

Your I-centricity is a curse you were born with that you inherited from your parents and will never escape, but you can be aware of it and learn how to control it. This will let you show up in a connected way that cuts through the noise and ensures you stand out from your competitors. You'll be seen by your future clients, which will help build your business – consistently and with ease.

WHY YOUR CURRENT MESSAGE
AND APPROACH SUCKS

Now that you know what being I-centric is and why it's holding you back from growing your business, we can start to look at specific ways your I-centricity is showing up in your communications and how to transform them.

All the activities you've been told to do by the gurus and other business coaches are centred around leading with yourself and putting yourself at the centre of how you show up. You've even been told to demonstrate your 'expertise' and 'be an authority'. What's wrong with this, I hear you wonder. It feels inauthentic for you, doesn't it? That's because when you show up in this way – share content that talks about your expertise and demonstrates your knowledge through so-called 'value' posts – you get a handful of likes, your mum's your biggest fan (thanks, Mum!) and you're getting very little conversion to clients. You've known for a while something wasn't quite right, but you just couldn't put your finger on exactly what it was. But as you're reading this, it's making sense, isn't it?

One of the least effective, yet widely followed practices in the business world is the practice of creating an 'I-help' statement to explain what you do. The problem with the I-help statement is that it's about YOU, not the people you're trying to connect with. The I-help sentence starts with the word 'I', which subconsciously tells the other person that what they're about to hear is about you, not them. And because they're I-centric too, they immediately switch off. No one cares about you unless you can tell them why they should in the way that is most meaningful to them, and what is most meaningful to them is THEM.

Let's look at some examples:

- **I-centric way:** I help coaches create content that connects and builds their business. (Boring!)

Versus

- **Connected way:** Master the art of creating content that connects and you'll have an abundance of people to serve. (Intriguing!)

What about:

- **I-centric way:** I help health professionals do more of the work they love without burning out. (Heard it before...)

Versus

- **Connected way:** Health professionals come to me when they want the tools to empower themselves to do the work they love in a way that nourishes them – without burning out. (Shut up and take my money!)

Or this:

- **I-centric way:** I teach individuals and couples how to create a fulfilling relationship. (So vanilla.)

Versus

- **Connected way:** Individuals and couples create a deeply intimate and fulfilling relationship with both themselves and each other when we work together on their communication and confidence. (The piece of the puzzle I've been missing!)

Which type is more appealing and creates curiosity within you? The I-centric way or the Connected way?

(I rest my case, Your Honour…)

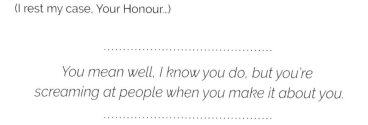

You mean well, I know you do, but you're screaming at people when you make it about you.

Your I-centricity is killing your business and your ability to have a greater impact, and it rears its ugly head most in HOW you are communicating with others – online and offline.

When you show up on social media and make comments to other people, I know you think you're being engaging and helpful, but most of the time you're not. How do I know? Consider this. How often do people reach out to you after seeing your content or a comment you made? Not often? Then what you're doing isn't engaging or helpful in their perception.

Here's an example of what you might be doing in an attempt to 'help', but is in fact repelling potential clients.

This post was made by a person on my friends list. I made a simple and encouraging comment acknowledging that he shared the post and thanking him for sharing his wisdom.

He came back and tried to school me on what he knows about how to graduate up concentric spheres, but I didn't ask for this, nor was I interested. Furthermore, by trying to 'educate' me on what he knows, he assumed that he knows more than me. Whether he does or doesn't is irrelevant at this connection point. It's very off-putting when people offer help or try to educate you when you haven't asked to be helped or educated. It is so important in business and life that you identify a need before you offer a solution. Have you experienced something similar? Have you commented on someone's post, then been taken aback and overwhelmed by how they kept trying to tell you more? Or maybe you secretly thought, 'What a know-it-all.'

You do your own version of this.

Here are some more examples of people attempting to be helpful, but actually repelling their audience – take a look to see if you do something similar:

This individual made a post about her best sales week, I congratulated her, then she said, 'Love to share how you could have as much fun as I am! She thought she was being helpful in wanting to share how she had her best sales week, but she was also assuming I'm not having fun (or my best sales week). When you assume, you make an ASS out of U and ME.

This person sent me a direct message because he genuinely thinks that helping people invest in real estate is going to be life-changing, and he wants to share with as many people as he can. But in reaching out and asking if I'd like to create the life of my dreams, he is assuming I am NOT living my dream and that I don't already have an investment strategy.

Another poster shared a quote by someone famous. I said, 'Wise words', and she then tried to tell me I'd like her TikTok... No doubt she wanted to be helpful, and maybe she shares lots of wise quotes on her TikTok, but again, assuming is not the way to connect online or in person.

Now you've seen these examples, have a think about how you might be doing something similar – or even exactly the same. Do you often make comments because you want to share what you know and be helpful? And can you now see that because no one asked for it, it is disconnecting you from other people?

This is YOU being I-centric. Yes, YOU do this. Which turns people OFF you. When you make comments to people and try to tell them what you know, you think you're being helpful. But you are NOT. You respect your audience, and as you try to show them all you know, you think your display of knowledge is flourishing. But your audience thinks you're up yourself, and they become subtly depressed from reading your 'screaming words of wisdom'.

This is costing you business. You repel potential clients when you do this. You do your own version of this and it's because of your I-centricity. I know you mean well. I know this is hard to take.

Want to attract more clients with ease? Stop speaking AT people and start leaving them feeling SEEN. Then, you don't have to sell to people. Then, they will naturally WANT to work with you because they feel connected to you. You have a choice. You can keep doing what you're doing and struggle to have consistent clients, or grow beyond your income ceiling each month.

FROM I-CENTRIC TO CONNECTION

You've been wasting a lot of time and energy online trying to build your business because you tell yourself that 'some action' is better than no action, but it's not bringing you results and now you know why. Your I-centricity gets in your way.

You're overworked, overwhelmed and lacking simplicity, which means you don't achieve the results you know you're capable of, and you keep reinventing the wheel because you think your strategy is the problem. Now you can see it's not so much WHAT strategy, but HOW you've been executing it that keeps disconnecting you from potential clients.

....

Stop spinning your wheels on social media. Stop doing more things. Instead, shift your I-centric nature to Connection. Then you will do LESS, but have MORE clients to serve.

....

Here's the thing. You're never (yes, never) going to get rid of your I-centricity. It is as much a part of you as your heart and brain are. The first step to growing your business and having consistency is being aware of your I-centric nature, because you can't transform what you don't acknowledge. Once you're aware of your I-centricity, you can catch yourself being I-centric and learn better ways to connect and communicate with others. Ways that are about both you and them, so that even in your natural state of I-centricity you can create connection that leaves your target audience feeling seen, which is what converts them to clients you serve. It's about less push, more magnetic pull.

Getting more by doing less

Gemma had been in business for over ten years and was consistently bringing in around 20,000 dollars per month. From the outside, it looked like her business was working. Except it wasn't working, because getting that 20,000 dollars a month left her exhausted. She was doing all the things she had been told to do: create content, post daily, give away free lead magnets, email her list every week, and add new friends and connections to her social media platforms to keep building her audience. She was pouring her time and energy into her business, but her return did not match her output. Gemma had a higher pain threshold than most people in that she was very action and task focused, so she could do more in an hour than most. This meant she was getting a lot more done than the average business owner, which was partly why she was bringing in 20,000 dollars a month. But this was not the most efficient or effective way for her to maintain her business, let alone grow it. Just because you *can* do more, doesn't mean you *should*.

Gemma couldn't scale her business because her time was 'maxed out'. She couldn't fit one more thing into the hours she worked because she was already over-delivering within them. What Gemma needed to do was capitalise on what she had already created, so that she could do less but receive more. It wasn't *what* she was doing that was the problem. It was *how* she was doing it that was stopping her from getting maximum return for her efforts. Meaning that instead of adding more friends to her network and sharing

more content, she just needed better quality content – content
that wasn't I-centric. Content that would connect with more of the
people already in her audience, and therefore capitalise more on
her time. So that instead of sharing five pieces of content to get a
return of one client, she could share less often but, when she did
share, all her content would convert to one or multiple clients.

When Gemma learned how to stop being I-centric and actually
connect, she started doing fewer hours. Her monthly revenue grew
because her ability to meaningfully connect converted more clients,
but required less activity and less time. Her audience felt seen, and
in turn saw her authenticity and uniqueness. Now more people in
her network are converting to clients consistently, and she doesn't
have to do anything extra. In fact, she does less!

Key insights

- The dream of having an easy life by creating a business can turn into a nightmare of struggle and stress. In reality, it isn't as easy as those gurus make it look.

- WHAT you're doing to grow your business isn't so much the problem; it's HOW you're doing it that's slowing your growth.

- You were born I-centric and so don't naturally possess connected communication skills, but you can learn them.

- You think you're being helpful when you give advice, but if someone isn't paying you for that advice your helpfulness is interpreted as you being a know-it-all. This disconnects you from potential clients and stops you from making more sales.

- Your I-help statement is I-centric; it's about you, not about others. People don't care about you unless you can tell them why they should. You do this by talking about what's most meaningful to them – which is THEM.

CHAPTER 2

Falling back in love with your business & life

For two years, Isabella went from coaching program to coaching program trying to find a way to grow her business in a logical and sustainable way that aligned with her values of how she wanted to show up in the world. She had quit her nine-to-five job, and along with it the comfort of the golden handcuffs and the six-figure income, to go all in and grow her career as a relationship coach.

When she came to me she had clients trickling in, but not consistently. She didn't have control or certainty over the flow of new clients, which meant she didn't have consistent and predictable revenue. She was in the feast or famine trap. One month she was winning, the next month she was stressing over whether she'd have enough money coming in. (I'm sure you can relate.)

This was putting incredible pressure on Isabella's personal life. She had given up many things that were important to her, like regular exercise, yoga and quality time with her partner. She was chained to her computer screen as she desperately tried to grow her business – with very little reward. Isabella told me that she was watching her savings account shrink with every passing month. She realised that the business coaching programs she had already tried were missing the most crucial element to long-term success: how to connect and build *real* relationships with potential clients – the true lifeblood of any business. Yes, those programs had said they would teach lead generation, but once she signed up, she quickly realised that what was promised and what was delivered didn't match up. She was left with more questions about how to grow a business than before she started.

....

Isabella was exhausted from putting a lot of activity into her business every day, but getting very little results for her efforts. She was also watching her personal life be consumed by work. Can you relate?

....

In addition to serving the clients she did have, Isabella was also trying to find new ones by getting on social media and trawling the online world for people who looked like they might be in her target audience. But this wasn't converting to clients for her. She was actually playing a guessing game, as she had no way to determine if the people she was connecting with had the problem she helps with and whether they were seeking a solution.

As a result, she spent hours every day looking for new friends and connections. She shared content like a hose that was spraying and praying on her audience, but which wasn't engaging with people or converting them to clients. When she did have a sales call she was using a script that left her feeling like a sleazy salesperson. She knew that relying on referrals was not an empowering or secure way to scale her business, but she also didn't know what else to do to generate consistent revenue without selling her soul to the social media machine.

If you're like Isabella, and think you have a lead generation problem (not enough potential clients coming in), and/or a sales problem (not converting enough of the people you do have conversations with), then you're barking up the wrong tree.

....

You don't have a lead gen and sales problem.
You have a connection problem.

....

Once Isabella learned how to control her I-centricity and how to connect with the right people – ones who were actually looking for help – she grew her business rapidly. In just three months she grew her monthly revenue by 125%, and fell back in love with growing her business. It became fun! She also was able to go back to doing things she loved in her personal life, like taking regular yoga classes, and saw that looking after herself literally grew her business. All it took was connection to herself and others.

ALWAYS IDENTIFY A NEED BEFORE
YOU OFFER A SOLUTION

One of my mentors taught me an invaluable lesson in business, which was to always identify a need before you offer a solution. I'm certain you aren't identifying a need before you offer a solution when you're on social media. From unsolicited direct messages offering free and paid offers, to sharing content about what you want to say instead of what your audience wants to hear, to even just the way you're commenting on and engaging with other people's content, you're probably projecting yourself and what you have to offer onto people. And when they inevitably reject your advances, you're left feeling ashamed and questioning whether you have what it takes to grow your business or if anyone actually wants what you offer.

It's not your offer that's the problem. It's that you're unintentionally projecting yourself onto others because you've been told to 'be an authority' online, but this is disconnecting you from potential clients.

Those who actually have authority don't need to push it onto others; it's a given. When you try to show you're an 'expert' with your content and post 'helpful' comments on other people's content – when you start educating them on what you know about what they shared – what you're really doing is projecting your expertise and knowledge onto someone who hasn't yet asked for it. Secretly, they'll think you're a know-it-all and won't want to know you at all (yes, there's a play on words there!). The key is knowing how to catch your I-centricity before you act and turn it into a connection approach that leaves your audience feeling seen.

Then you experience less push and more magnetic pull.

FROM DISCONNECTED TO INSPIRED

Mastering the art of connection means unlearning a way of being that you've been taught from birth about how to interact with other people. But what's your alternative? You can keep doing what you're doing, which is leaving you feeling disconnected and exhausted from a lot of activity that gives very little return. Or you can be open to walking the path to connection, which leads to having more people to serve.

Here's how the journey unfolds if you choose the latter path.

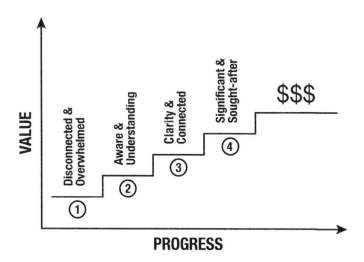

Stage 1: Disconnected & overwhelmed

You launched your business so you could have freedom and spend more time doing things you love, but it's left you overwhelmed and feeling disconnected from yourself and your loved ones.

At the disconnected and overwhelmed stage, you've been trying to grow your business beyond your current level for a long time. Unlike many other people in your position, you haven't given up – *yet*. Here you are, still going, still giving it your best shot, believing that one day soon things are going to turn around and get better.

Except you've been telling yourself this same story for a while now and it hasn't gotten better, has it? If you're at this stage, then the rest of your life is suffering because you've given up things such as looking after your health or spending time with your loved ones. Your business has become all-consuming. If you keep going like this, you may end up burning out. You keep trying, though. You keep doing the same things every day, hoping they will move you forward, but you're still stuck in the same position.

You know how Einstein said insanity is doing the same thing over and over again and expecting a different result? You're smiling and nodding because it makes sense, but here you are playing out your own version of insanity in your attempts to grow your business. Doing long hours just to find clients and work on your business shouldn't be this hard, should it?

....

The love and enthusiasm you once had for growing your business and serving has started fading away. The spark still exists deep inside, but you know if something doesn't change soon that spark is going to completely die.

....

You're pretending that everything is okay, but inside you feel empty and confused about what to do next because you believe you've tried it all.

Your personal life has been suffering because you have no spare time, and you feel ashamed and embarrassed to tell the people closest to you that you're struggling to grow your business.

Your confidence is fading.

But, there's an inner voice speaking to you. Some days it's like a quiet whisper, others it's a loud scream.

Your inner wisdom knows you can fix this, and you're searching for the answers to take your next step. You become aware that something isn't right and you're ready to make a change.

Stage 2: Aware & understanding

When you reach the aware stage, you realise that a lot of programs you've tried already have just regurgitated similar strategies. None of them really teach people *how* to deeply connect with others in an authentic way that also converts them to clients. You see how you've been left alone to execute the knowledge you're given, which means you're never sure if you're doing it 'right'.

This is what is fundamentally missing from the business coaching industry – you're given information, but no mentor is in the car with you while you drive your business in real-time. When you learn to drive a car you might read some instructions and do some online training, but when you first get behind the wheel you have an instructor sitting beside you. You need that when it comes to growing your business, too. You realise that just knowing more 'stuff' isn't going to help you grow. What's been missing from everything you've tried so far is that you haven't had your mentor with you, in real-time, while you apply what you've learned.

This is partly why Isabella had her record-breaking month just four weeks after she started working with me and continued to grow her business consistently. I didn't just teach her more 'stuff'; I executed with her.

Is this where you are right now? Are you aware of and do you understand what the problem *actually* is and what you need to do to grow?

You know that if you want to have something you've never had, you're going to have to do something you've never done (Einstein wasn't kidding, hey?).

....

*Even though you place a high value
on learning, you know it's time to
turn that learning into earning.*

....

You realise that you can't just learn more 'stuff'. You have to execute the things you learn – and execute consistently – because that's what creates results and keeps building more results. Next time you sign on with a mentor, you will ensure they execute with you, not just give you more information.

Even though you love connecting with people and value quality relationships, you realise that your current approach isn't translating into consistent clients or growing your business past your income ceiling. And you're smart enough and humble enough to know that you don't know it all.

You're ready to learn how to drop your I-centricity, meaningfully connect, and apply the work consistently to get consistent results.

Stage 3: Clarity & connected

Once you've learned how to identify your I-centricity and transform it to connection behaviours, you are clear and confident and other people start to notice you a lot more. You leave other people feeling seen, they see you as the go-to expert, and you've positioned yourself as someone others want to work with.

When you're connecting with your audience, they choose you over your competitors. Your content is more appealing because it's about your audience, not you. You clearly and confidently initiate, connect and lead conversations with the right people – people who have the problem you help with – and they thank you for your authenticity and want to work with you because of it.

When you are connected to your audience, you can do less but attract more clients who want to work with you. You're magnetic, and what you have to say and share, both online and in 'real life', attracts more people to you.

This is mastering the art of connection. It will give you an abundance of people to serve – consistently.

Stage 4: Significant & sought-out leader

Finally, you become inspired and energised by your mission and by serving humanity again. Your business has become a joy, and you jump out of bed eager to start your day and connect with and serve your clients. You've created a playground for getting what you want, which is to have wider impact, the freedom and flexibility you dreamed of, and appreciation from clients whom you love working with. You have this with ease and flow in your heart and mind, as well as in your business.

....

You have clarity in your vision. You value what you bring to the world through your service. Your message connects, and how you connect has become less I-centric – now you and your target audience are aligned.

....

You've become sought after. You're speaking with fewer people directly, but they're the right people who convert consistently. You're doing less outbound lead generation and have more inbound clients seeking you out for the significant impact they know you can give them. You're in control and have reclaimed your personal life because you don't have to work such long hours. The freedom you got into business for has finally started to become your reality.

You believe in yourself and give yourself permission to grow to the next level.

....

*Ask yourself honestly: where are you currently at,
and where would you like to be?*

....

DEEP WORK THAT TRANSFORMS ALL AREAS

One small shift can make a huge difference. Once you become aware of the I-centricity that's been running you and the way you show up in the world – with everyone, not just in your business – your entire life transforms.

When you go from I-centric communication to connected communication, your business grows. And when your business grows, you create the freedom you were looking for when you first launched. You can spend that extra time on your emotional wellbeing, and with your family and loved ones. You can focus on your health again, which connects you with yourself and energises you. This energy allows you to serve more clients and have more impact, and therefore more money.

You'll become more self-aware and understand yourself on a much deeper level. You'll love and appreciate yourself for who you are and all that you've already achieved. Your vision will be clear again as you can see what you're truly capable of creating for your future. You'll improve your communication skills, not only in your business but in all areas of your life. This leads to a shift in how others respond to you, which energises you and helps you feel fulfilled and purposeful. You start attracting clients who are more aligned with your values and deeply appreciate the transformation you offer. This energises you because you're working with soul-clients instead of feeling like you have to say yes to anyone just to pay your bills.

All this happens because you have learned how to be less I-centric and more connected to yourself and others.

Now you've identified where you want to get to, it's time to look at how to get there. It's not that you don't have what it takes. It's just that you don't know yet how to be less I-centric and more connected in your approach so that people are actually interested in you. Connection is the source of your business life because it's what attracts and converts more people for you to serve. Without it, your business won't survive, let alone flourish.

That's what you'll learn in the next part of this book and, in doing so, completely open up your business and your life.

From drain to gain

Patrick had spent over twelve months away from his business after experiencing deep grief over the death of three loved ones, all of whom died within a short space of time. When he reached out to me to see if I could help him bring his coaching business back to life, he had done the inner work to process his grief, but lacked the confidence to go back out into the world and share his gifts.

For Patrick, it was like starting his business all over again. He was feeling disconnected from potential clients. He was overwhelmed with not knowing how to get started again. How could he work efficiently and effectively, so that he didn't use his precious time and energy on things that wouldn't give him a return? He had a family and didn't want them to miss out on quality time with him. Patrick knew the key to getting his business up and going again was to have hands-on help, rather than trying to figure things out on his own.

The first thing we worked on was getting him reconnected to himself, and the love and enthusiasm he had for serving others and making an impact through his business. Through mindset work, we discovered that his lack of confidence was connected to his perceived failures in previous businesses. When we looked at each of these so-called failures, Patrick found that he had also had success in those failures. He was able to reframe his story and didn't feel there was something missing from his capabilities anymore. To ignite his love for serving, and so he could attract new clients, we did an exercise that got him clear and aligned to his vision again. This energised him to want to connect with others and serve them. Once we defined a strategy for him to create content that replaced his I-centric message with one about the people he wanted to connect with, he started booking sales. Within four weeks of working together, he closed new clients.

Now clients are seeking Patrick out because his message and content is about them. It's no longer an I-centric message about him, and therefore it's resonating with his clients. Patrick's love and enthusiasm for his life and business have returned.

Key insights

- You don't have a lead gen or sales problem. You have a connection problem.

- If you've sacrificed parts of your life that are important to you, like exercise or socialising with loved ones, because your business has become all-consuming, then it's time to do something about it – now, before you burn out.

- Standard business growth programs and coaching you've tried in the past have given you information, but they lacked a mentor who could guide you through the execution phase. This is largely why you still don't have the results you've been trying to create. Much like when you learn to drive a car and have your instructor with you, you need your mentor with you when you're growing your business to ensure you correctly execute the techniques you've learned.

- Once you know how to identify your I-centric behaviours and transform them into connection behaviours, your target audience will seek you out over your competitors.

- You naturally become more confident when you know how to connect.

PART 2

CONNECTION

CHAPTER 3

Master your message

It's not about you. It's about them.

If you're in business, you have something to say. But is anyone listening?

What are you sharing on social media and, more importantly, *why are you sharing it?* Do you share your content because you think it's valuable to your audience, or because you want to share something and get the dopamine dose that a bunch of likes gives you? A quick scroll of your newsfeed and you'll see I-centricity is leading in almost every single post. From 'I' and 'My' statements to over-shares about people's personal lives, social media is being treated like a diary instead of being used in the way it was intended – to connect. The same thing is happening from a business perspective, and if you take a look at your content you'll likely see that you keep talking about you and your business in the context of what you want, what you have to offer and what you have achieved, rather than in the context of the consumer and what they are interested in – which is themselves.

Do your posts start with 'I', 'My client', 'We are proud to…'? Then you've made your message about you rather than your audience.

Have you shared a testimonial and added some verbiage about what your client or you achieved, rather than talking about what's possible for your audience?

Do you over-share about your cat, dog, kids, what you had for break-fast? Can you see that those posts get more engagement than any of your business-related content? What's that telling you? That you just don't know how to connect in business. If you could create compelling business content, you'd be getting engagement through that, not your cute cat and avocado on toast posts.

Are you sharing multiple posts or emails every week about what you want to show people, rather than asking them about what *they* want to know and see, and then creating content based on their answers?

If so, you've made your message solely about you rather than about your audience, and in doing so you've become part of the online noise. The people you're trying to connect with and turn into clients are scrolling straight past your content, or not opening your emails and not hearing your message, because you have failed to make it about them.

The good news is that you can easily change this. Because most businesses will keep doing what they're doing by making their message about them, rather than learn how to master their message and make it about what their audience wants, you'll have your market share and stand out from your competitors when you make your message about your audience rather than you.

FROM WIRED TO INSPIRED

As a human being, you're hardwired to automatically and constantly be thinking about yourself; speaking for yourself and about yourself, and seeking to get from any connection and communication what you want and need with very little consideration for your audience. This is the nature of being human, and we are all the same. You are speaking AT people rather than WITH them – and they're doing the same to you.

From the moment you're born and throughout your childhood, you are *not* taught how to truly connect with others. As a baby you're taught that the world is about you. If you cry, wink, gurgle or make any movement at all, you're showered with attention. You learn that the world revolves around you. As you move through your toddler years to your pre-teens, you experience life through your feelings, and relate to others and the world through the lens of how it all affects you. You have very little thought about how others are experiencing life.

You then go into adolescence, and by this stage life has become increasingly challenging. You're navigating the hormones surging within you and the emotions they create, while simultaneously trying to understand the external world and find your place in society as adulthood knocks on your door.

By default, your mind is constantly thinking about you, what you want, what you need and your desires. In fact, when you aren't focused on solving a defined problem, ninety-five per cent of the time you're thinking about YOURSELF. And every other individual on this earth is also thinking about THEMSELVES.

So now, every single day, we have close to eight billion people roaming the world talking AT one another rather than WITH each other. It's no wonder we're at war with ourselves and each other.

This is why your message and content fall on deaf ears. But once you transform your I-centricity and master your message, you'll be speaking WITH your audience rather than AT them. You will connect with more people, which makes it possible for you to have the impact you know you were born to have.

....

Your message is the meeting point between your heart and mind and the hearts and minds of the people you'd love to serve.

....

Your message reflects the gift you have to offer your clients. Your business message is also the entry point for your future clients to connect with you, and to know if they resonate with you and want to work with you. It is directly correlated to your inspired mission, which is ultimately what you want to have for yourself in this life as well as the gift you want to give others. Crafting your message is as much about your future clients as it is about you.

DON'T MAKE YOUR MESS YOUR MESSAGE

There's a reason you choose to serve in the way you do; it's not a random decision. You have experienced a challenge, solved its associated problems, and now want to share your wisdom with others so you can create impact and change lives. You might help others with grief because you've experienced it or help your clients to create a loving relationship because you were able to do that. Whatever you do or however you serve, it's because you've had a life-changing experience and you now want to help others achieve the same breakthrough.

This doesn't mean that your message should be consistently focused on your past experiences, your 'hard-luck' story or what you've done in your life to achieve great things. Despite what you've been told by numerous coaches, learned through programs you've taken or heard people say on social media, it's not wise to make your message all about you.

For example, the weight-loss coach shouldn't be posting their own 'before and after' photos every week and telling their audience about how they lost the weight. It gets very old and very boring very quickly. They also shouldn't be sharing photos of themselves eating a meal and talking about their relationship with food and how they now coach people all over the world to eat as well as they do. Your story gives you some credibility, yes, but it isn't enough to instil trust in your audience and convince them that you're the best person to help them. When you lead with yourself, you're likely to be so far ahead of your audience in terms of results that what you have seems almost unobtainable to them. People also get sick of hearing all about you because no one cares about you unless you can tell them why they should in terms of what they care about most – which is them.

Nor should you be trying to directly sell in every piece of content or email that you share. Don't drop links in every post or tell people to send you a message for more information. Your audience will start to feel sold to, and actually stop consuming your content because they've come to expect a hard pitch in every post.

But why does everyone else do it, I hear you say?

Don't fall into the trap of thinking that just because 'everyone' is doing something that it's working. It's not. For example, there are an estimated 5,842,000 coaches in the world right now and only four per cent of them consistently make 10,000 dollars or more per month. Most of them aren't coaching full time, and in fact their coaching business is a side hustle that they're trying to get up and going and make their main thing. But it won't ever be their main thing, because they've subscribed to what the masses are doing – which isn't working – instead of connecting with the master that they truly are. They've made their message about them and their own 'mess' rather than the people they want to connect with.

....

Your message is found in your mess, but don't make your mess your message.

....

You've got a mess of stories, experiences, challenges and lessons you've learned over your lifetime that have led you to show up and serve your people in an inspired way. But that should not be your main message when you're trying to attract and retain clients.

You know those posts that start with: 'So many new followers, so thought I'd share a little about me,' and then dive into the author's life story and how they can now coach you? That's an I-centric message.

Ever seen stories in which people tell you there's a 'New Post!', then try to direct you to something they shared on their profile? That's an I-centric message.

What about 'Invitation to work with me' posts and emails calling out the type of client the poster wants, followed by a pretend scarcity statement like 'Limited spots available'. That's an I-centric message.

Then there's content promising to help you achieve an outcome that's littered with 'I' statements. That's an I-centric message.

Photos of half-naked bodies to try and capture attention in the scroll. That's an I-centric message.

Testimonial posts that are photos or videos of the client saying something about the service provider, but nothing about their audience and what they can achieve. That's an I-centric message.

How does this type of content make you feel?

Annoyed? Disengaged? Bored?

That's because the message is I-centric. And even though you mean well, you've likely done one of these or you're doing something similar, and you don't realise it because your intentions are pure.

....

*You have a powerful mission to serve this world,
but if you don't craft your message in a way that
is authentic, and meaningful to the people you're
looking to serve, then it will forever go unheard.*

....

WHAT ABOUT ME?

You might now be wondering where you fit into the equation if you're not supposed to make your message about you.

To understand this a bit better, let's look at the science of it and the work of Sigmund Freud, the founder of the clinical method of psychoanalysis and a pioneer in psychology. Freud believed what is most important to every person is the Self, and what we all have in common is the desire to understand ourselves and know ourselves.

....

*The Self is central to your business message, but
it's not just your Self that must be considered
when crafting or sharing that message.*

....

You need to know the Self of those you want to serve.

When you leave people with the sense that you understand them, they inherently believe you have the solution to their problems.

When this happens, there is very little selling involved and a whole lot more serving.

So, your job is to know your audience better than they know their Self, and to speak to them through your message so they can connect with what you're saying and feel that you see them and understand them.

To leave people feeling seen, to show that you understand them and to influence their decision-making, you have to speak to a specific region of the brain. The pre-frontal cortex, also known as the 'executive centre' of the brain, is the region responsible for higher-level cognitive skills like objective reasoning, planning and focus.

Gareth Cook, a Pulitzer Prize-winning journalist and editor for *Scientific American*, effectively sums up how to use the Self to connect with others in the article 'Why we are wired to connect'. He says:

> *'Given that we tend to think of the self as the thing that separates us from others – that allows us to know how we are different and how to walk our own path – it would be surprising if this same medial pre-frontal region was involved in allowing the beliefs of others to influence our own. But this is exactly what we have seen in several studies. The more active the medial pre-frontal region is when someone is trying to persuade you of something (e.g. to wear sunscreen every day) the more likely you'll be to change your tune and start using sunscreen regularly. Rather than being a hermetically sealed vault that separates us from others, our research suggests that*

the self is more of a Trojan horse, letting in the beliefs of others, under the cover of darkness and without us realising it. This socially influenced self helps to ensure that we'll have the same kind of beliefs and values as those of the people around us and this is a great catalyst for social harmony.[1]

This means that to engage with your audience through your message, you should aim to permeate their beliefs (not yours), so you can connect with their heart and mind. You do this by making your message about *them*, not *you*.

INFLUENCE, DON'T LEAD

What does leadership mean to you? Your definition most likely conjures up images of a leader at the front of the crowd paving the way for those they are responsible for. Leaders in corporations manage people, leaders in politics manage people and outcomes for their constituents, leaders in your family (typically the parents) manage people. Leadership is about managing.

Yet you are not here to manage your clients, but to help them awaken to what is already within them, to help them shine a light on what's currently in the dark.

---

1   Gareth Cook, "Why We Are Wired to Connect," Scientific American, October 22, 2013, https://www.scientificamerican.com/article/why-we-are-wired-to-connect/

....

You're here to be influential in helping your clients and customers access their own inner wisdom.

....

A 2015 study conducted at a premier European business and law school, ESADE, demonstrated that people with leadership ability, no matter their position or personality profile, shared a single trait in common: the ability to influence their own nervous systems and, by extension, the nervous systems of others.

These findings suggest that genuine influence does not depend upon having a 'leadership' position or authority, and that true leadership involves influencing others to connect with what you have to say.

The most effective way to influence someone is to speak in terms of what's most meaningful to them, which is THEM, not you.

You're stuck in I-centricity.

You're I-centric.

As we learned earlier, 'centric' means 'concentrated about or directed to a centre activity', and when we bring the words 'I' and 'centric' together – I-centric – it means 'you at the centre'. This is your modus operandi, and it's a problem when it comes to making authentic connections with people you'd love to serve because it does the very opposite for you – it disconnects you from them.

Neuroscience tells us that you stay stuck in your I-centric way because you perceive that it's beneficial for you. That's because when you're being I-centric, you feel that you're 'right'. This causes your brain to produce a high level of dopamine – a neurotransmitter associated with reward that reinforces your desire to repeat that pattern. While this addictive I-centric pattern makes you feel powerful and drives you to crave more of it, this power-over pattern can also push you away from others because they find your addiction egotistical and arrogant.

Yes, you have a chemical addiction to being I-centric.

You're drowning out.

In the year 2000, the average attention span of an American was twelve seconds. Today, in 2022, it's around eight seconds, and when people are on social media it's as little as 1.8 seconds.

You have 1.8 seconds or less to capture and keep the attention of your target audience with your message, and your competition is fierce. There are sixty billion messages sent out across digital platforms every day; you and your audience are bombarded with messaging all day long.

Every time you pick up your smartphone you find an array of notifications to check and actions to take from your emails, texts, missed calls and social media platforms. You and your audience are overwhelmed by these notifications, and often miss them because of their sheer number. You can't assume that just because you sent an email or published a social media post that your audience saw it, let alone read it.

How many times a day do you stop and consume someone else's ENTIRE piece of content? Not often, right? Every time I've asked my clients this question, they've told me that it's under five times a day. So too for the people *you're* trying to connect with and serve. They aren't seeing you as much as you think they are.

Your I-centric communication style isn't helping you to overcome the obstacle of capturing and keeping the attention of your audience.

HOW I-CENTRICITY SHOWS UP IN YOUR COMMUNICATION

How many times a day do you start a sentence with 'I'?

The word 'I' is the most used pronoun in the English language. It's also ranked the tenth most frequently used word in English, right up there with words like 'the' and 'be'. This means you're probably using 'I' frequently in your communication, which means you're making your communication all about you.

When you start a sentence with the word 'I', it immediately tells the people you're trying to communicate with that what they're about to hear or read is about you, not them, so they switch off. You'll be doing this on autopilot, and most of the time you don't realise how much you're saying 'I'. But as you read this your inner wisdom knows that it's true. What you're reading here makes complete sense.

Your message is full of I-centric communication, and so it often goes unheard. Since your modus operandi is to be I-centric, when someone asks you about what you do you will automatically revert to an 'I-help' statement.

You know what I'm talking about. 'I help business owners to blah blah.' 'I help singles to blah blah.' 'I help leaders to blah blah.' The 'I-help' statement is plastered all over most service providers' communication material, 'About' blurb and social media pages – including yours.

I-help is I-centric and generic, and when you use it you're not being seen for the unique service provider that you are. This is why you look like just another salesperson in your target audience's inbox and newsfeed. Since no one cares about you unless you can tell them why they should in the context of them, your 'I-help' statement is causing you to lose potential clients.

Let's imagine you're a coach who works with health professionals. You set up systems to streamline core elements in their business, such as their marketing, so that they reduce burnout and fall in love with their work again. As a result, rather than being chained to their business, your clients have more money and more time to do things in their personal life.

Now imagine you're at a friend's barbecue and you know hardly anyone there. You're stuck making classic small talk with people, which inevitably leads to the question, 'What do you do?' Automatically, you say, 'I help health professionals to do more of the work they love in the way they love to do it,' because that is your default I-centric I-help statement and you're focused on showing others how passionate you are about helping them to love their work again.

But you see the other person's eyes glaze over, and you soon part ways and never see each other again.

But what if that person had been the perfect-fit client for you – a health professional on the verge of burnout with broken systems in their business that are keeping them stuck in a pile of admin?

Unfortunately, you lost them at 'I'...

All they heard was you giving health professionals more work to do, which is overwhelming for somebody pushed to the edge of a nervous breakdown by their immense workload. So now you've lost a potential new client. And they've missed out on a chance to work with you and finally set up systems to reduce their burnout and reclaim their wellbeing and their life.

And what if, a few weeks later, they hit their peak of anxiety, experience burnout and are diagnosed with a debilitating mental illness? An illness that keeps them away from their business indefinitely. This could have been avoided if you knew how to communicate in a way that connected with them. In a way that created clarity for them. In a way that allowed them to see that you had a solution that would create the freedom they so desperately desired and needed.

....

Your default, I-centric 'I-help' statement is where you should start transforming your message to communicate clearly how you can best serve your people, which then leads to more people hearing you and becoming clients whom you serve.

....

THE TRUST FRAMEWORK™

It's time for a better way to share your message, a way that allows you to be seen by your target audience and truly connect so that you have more people to serve. You need to replace your 'I-help' statement with the TRUST Framework™.

The TRUST Framework™ is a mnemonic acronym that's easy to remember and will help retrain your brain out of its default 'I-help' mode and put you in control of how you communicate. TRUST stands for:

T – Target Audience
R – Reach
U – You
S – Solution
T – Transformation

The TRUST Framework™ can be used in any setting. At that barbecue, in conversations on social media, at speaking events, when networking, and even in the 'About' section on your website and profiles.

It works because you start your sentence about your audience, not you, so that your audience immediately begins to pay attention. You give a high-level overview of what your solution is so that your audience understand what makes you unique. Most importantly, you offer clarity on what life looks like for them after they start working with you. This is important, because people don't care how they get a result as much as they care about having the result. You create a picture of what the future looks like for your audience, and that is what we're all interested in knowing.

Now grab a pen and paper to complete the following short, but powerful exercise on how to master your message so that you have more clients to serve.

Step 1: Target audience

Who are the people you serve?

It's important that you immediately speak directly to and about the individual/s you serve, so that you capture their attention.

Remember the 1.8 second rule – lead with what's important to THEM.

By starting your message with WHO, rather than with 'I', you capture and keep the attention of your audience.

You may be speaking with someone you don't think is part of your target audience, but you could be surprised. Starting your mes-sage with WHO will help capture the right listeners – even if you're unaware that they're listening.

Defining factors might be their job title, their mission, their role in life (mum, parents, and so on).

So, grab a pen now and jot down who you think is your target audience.

_____

_____

_____

_____

_____

_____

Step 2: Reach

This is the way your audience come to you – reach you – and what it expresses is the tangible doing action that makes it clear you are a service provider.

Suggestions include: 'come to', 'work with', 'seek out my services', 'connect with', 'engage'.

_____

_____

_____

Step 3: You

It's important to add YOU to the equation – it's about both you and them.

You are represented by the word 'me' or 'us'.

_____

_____

_____

Step 4: Solution

Sharing your high-level solution positions you in the marketplace and creates curiosity.

So describe your solution at a high level: the WHAT, not the HOW; the CONCEPT, not the PROCESS.

If you get weighed down by details, you'll lose your audience. Remember, they can't possibly appreciate the depth of what you offer – yet.

If you have a name for your offering, you can use that IF it is also practically clear. If it's ambiguous it won't capture attention. If it's hard to understand you will lose your audience.

Suggestions on how to share your solution: 'learn', 'unlock', 'discover'.

_____

_____

_____

Step 5: Transformation

Your audience care more about the OUTCOME than the process to get there.

Create the experience of that outcome for them with the transformation section.

What do they deeply want? That is how you describe the transformation you can make possible.

Here is what a TRUST message looks like – this example is from my own business:

'Entrepreneurs, coaches and consultants come to me to learn how to "master their message" and "create content that connects" so they consistently have an abundance of soul mate clients to serve.'

_____

_____

_____

Creating your message

1. Following the formula, plug in your words using the guidance from each section.
2. Create multiple versions of your message until you feel connected to the one that stands out the most.
3. Once complete, practice speaking your message.
4. Use your message in communication and watch how others respond to you – did the message connect? Did you notice people listening instead of seeing their eyes glaze over? If not, go back and repeat the process.

Once you use your TRUST message and see it connecting with your audience, you'll enjoy more connections and conversions from your communication.

Using your message

You could start by updating the 'About' section on your website or social media profiles, because I bet you've got an 'I-help' statement there.

When you use the TRUST Framework™, potential clients feel seen by you, and more of them will actually listen and learn about how you can help them. When people feel seen by you, they instinctively believe that you must have the solution to their problem. This means you'll be doing a whole lot less selling and much more serving.

You also stand out from your competitors, since most of them are using an I-centric 'I-help' statement. Now, instead of looking like another generic service provider, the unique gifts you have to offer are clear and obvious. More people in your market will choose you over a competitor.

This is especially important if your service is seen as a readily available commodity in a saturated market.

From commodity to connection

Brenda is an expert-turned-coach with a counselling practice as well as a coaching business. Both her service areas – counselling and coaching – are saturated markets where clients are spoiled for choice and the services are seen as a commodity readily available for consumption.

Brenda's strengths were not in the area of attraction, connection and conversion of new clients. She preferred to be serving, and that's where she found her joy, but she was wise enough to know that without effective client attraction a business isn't going to grow.

She felt she had tried it all. She had worked with marketing coaches and taken well-known programs from the so-called gurus, but nothing was getting her the results she wanted. What she wanted was less time doing outbound marketing, more time responding to potential clients who came directly to her, and more time being in service to those clients.

It was frustrating for Brenda because she knew she had something unique to offer compared with her competitors. She had done a lot more learning in her service area than most, and wanted to share this knowledge with more clients so she could have a bigger impact and change their lives.

Brenda wasn't sure how she could differentiate herself in the marketplace. She was using generic messaging that looked similar to her competitors' and she had an 'I-help' statement plastered everywhere. Her clients couldn't hear how she was different and why they should choose her because her message was just part of the noise. Brenda often felt that she was doing a lot of work trying to attract clients, but her income wasn't matching the time and energy she was spending on generating new clients.

Brenda worked with me to get clear on her message. She updated all her profiles using the TRUST Framework™, and now has more clients reaching out to her consistently because she made her message about them – which none of her competitors are doing.

Counselling and coaching are a service area where potential clients are saturated with choice, but now Brenda stands out from her competitors, and her message connects with the hearts and minds of the people she'd love to serve.

Key insights

- You were born I-centric and it's your default position for how you communicate, but you can learn to transform it and connect more strongly to attract more clients.

- Does your content start with 'I', 'My client', 'We are proud to...'? Then you've made your message about you, rather than your audience.

- The default 'I-help' statement you use when someone asks, 'What do you do?' is losing you potential clients because it's about you, not them.

- Use the TRUST Framework to craft a connected and converting message.

- Almost all your competitors are I-centric and share I-centric messages and content. When you learn how to master your message in a way that's about your audience, you will have a competitive edge.

CHAPTER 4

Soul mate clients

One of the most famous speeches in history is Martin Luther King Jr's 'I have a dream' speech, which he delivered in 1963. He was clear on his message, and he spoke it with clarity and conviction – but that isn't the only reason his message connected.

Martin Luther King's speech was a success because he was speaking to the right audience. He was speaking to people who wanted to hear what he had to say. Those people were problem aware and they wanted a solution. They were ready for change. Dr King was the messenger of hope and inspiration they needed to inspire them to take action and change their lives and the lives of generations to come.

Dr King was crystal clear on who his audience was, and he managed to gather them in one space to hear him share his message. He addressed a crowd of over 250,000 people, and his speech sparked a movement that helped create the Civil Rights Act of 1964 and the Voting Rights Act of 1965 – legislation that started to transform racial segregation in the United States.

If Dr King had turned up that day in 1963 and shared his message with the wrong crowd, or with very few people, then its impact would not have been so great. You are one person and you can effect change, but the larger your audience is, and the more of the right people are in it – people who want your message and will act on it – the greater your impact is going to be.

....

Like Martin Luther King Jr, you can only connect with your message and have impact when you share it with the right audience.

....

YOUR SCHOOL HALL

Remember when you were a child in primary school, and the assembly bell rang and everybody congregated in the school hall? The teacher on stage would start talking, and every student would sit still and listen to them as they shared their message.

Your social media profile, no matter which platform you use, is similar to a school hall.

You're on stage every time you share your message or a piece of content, but if you don't have the right students in your hall – that is, the right friends, connections or followers – then your message falls on deaf ears. You keep sharing content and wondering why you're getting little to no engagement or conversion and your mum is your biggest fan (thanks for the likes, Mum). Well, this is part of the reason why.

The issue is that you've been told to get on social media and add friends, connections or followers, but you've been playing a guessing game when it comes to exactly who you should add. As a result, your message and content aren't consistently converting to clients because the wrong people are listening.

....

No matter how good you think your message and content are, if you don't have the right audience then they're simply not going to convert to clients and your impact will be minimal.

....

STOP SPRAYING AND PRAYING

Everything you've been told about how to define your niche and find 'the right people' is generic, and when you follow these cookie cutter methods it contributes to why you don't have as many clients to serve as you'd like.

You keep adding friends and connections at random, and using demographics and psychographics that mean very little when it comes to practical application. You know the ones I'm talking about: 'What do they have for breakfast?', 'What do they watch on television?', 'Where do they want to be in five years?' and so on. You've answered all the customer avatar questions, created personas of your potential clients, hung the avatar sheet above your work desk, then opened up your social media platforms to find these people and...

You're even more lost and confused than when you first started.

You're guessing who your people are and taking a 'spray and pray' approach to adding friends and connections on social media. This is impeding your ability to fill your school hall with people who want what you've got and will convert to clients when they see your content.

It's not your fault.

You're doing as you were told and hoping that one day it will pay off. Except now you're tired, disappointed, drained and questioning yourself. You're wondering if you have what it takes to grow your business, and you even question if you've chosen the 'right' niche. You're starting to think your niche isn't profitable and it would be easier to go sell ice to Eskimos.

Here's what those so-called gurus haven't told you.

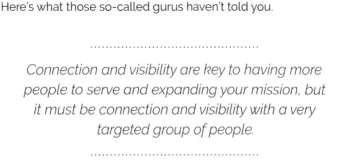

Connection and visibility are key to having more people to serve and expanding your mission, but it must be connection and visibility with a very targeted group of people.

Stop spraying and praying, and instead work on finding your '10%'.

FIND YOUR 10%

Not all the people in your target audience will buy from you. In fact, only 10% of those who fit the demographics and psychographics of your clients will actually buy from you. That's because, out of 100% of people who fit the characteristics of your target audience, only 10% are problem aware and solution seeking. Let's take a closer look.

Your 10% are broken down into two different buckets of people:

1. Three per cent are problem aware and seeking a solution right now.
2. Seven per cent are pain aware, but will seek a solution over time and convert later.

Right now, three per cent of your target market is problem aware and solution seeking. They will convert straight away if you know how to find them, identify them and get your message in front of them in a meaningful way. Another seven per cent of your target market are pain aware, but take longer to convert to clients because they need a little more education on the solution and a little more nurturing.

On average it takes around ten to fifteen organic touch points (non-paid advertising) to convert a potential client in your three per cent bucket, and even more if you're running paid ads. The people inside your seven per cent bucket may already be working on their problem with another business or mentor. These people are on the journey of growth, however, so when they finish with the service they're currently using to solve their problem, it's highly likely they will be looking for the next offer of help. This is the journey of evolution.

Think about it. Have you ever tried just one thing, worked with just one coach, taken just one course, to solve a problem? No. Like you, your future clients value learning and expansion and they're constantly looking for the next option on their journey of growth. So, next time you speak with someone who says, 'I'm currently working with someone to help me with XYZ…,' instead of assuming they'll *never* need your help, it's wise to bring them into your school hall and stay connected. You might just be the next person they choose on their learning journey.

....

Know and be visible to your 10% to grow your school hall with future clients who will actually buy from you. That's how you stand out from all the noise and make a profound connection, just like Martin Luther King Jr did.

....

WHO DO YOU WANT TO SERVE?

I truly believe that everyone deserves to be served. However, you're not going to be excited to serve every person who falls into your 10% target audience. Inside your 10% there are two buckets of different client types, and it's for you to choose where in the game you want to play and with whom.

Level 1-5 clients

People who fall into this bucket typically have limited awareness and understanding of the problems and solutions you specialise in.

Relative to your service delivery area, they typically haven't been on their learning journey for very long and serving them requires a lot more of your time, attention and energy. There are a lot of gaps in their knowledge, so they require more knowledge and a longer integration period to move forward. This might even cause you to feel drained or frustrated when serving them, unless you have systems in place to address these challenges.

Often, their mindset is also limited. They don't understand that the learning and expansion in your service area is a lifelong journey. Rather, they believe that your 'eight-week program' or simple solution should give them everything they'll ever need and solve all of their problems. And when it doesn't, they appear confused.

....

Level 1–5 clients invest in working with you because they're motivated by running away from the pain of the past or a problem in the present.

....

If you choose to focus on working with clients at this level, you have the benefit of a large pool to choose from and you play an important role in planting a seed of awareness in them that will later flourish into a beautiful bloom – if they choose to keep expanding their journey. The drawback is that you will have to go much slower in your approach, and you may not see fast or extensive progress.

Think about the clients you've served so far. Who have you worked with that fall into this category?

I had a client named Katherine who fell into this category. I remember a Saturday night when my phone started pinging over and over again and lighting up with Facebook notifications. Katherine was consuming my content and hitting 'like' on several pieces. We had a conversation in Messenger, and she booked a call for the following week. On the call Katherine required no selling at all. She told me she had already worked with seventeen different coaches to try to grow her business, and still didn't have a paying client. She wanted to start working with me immediately.

This was a red flag, and I should have heeded it and not signed her on to work with me. But at that time my desire to help everyone dominated my inner wisdom, which was telling me she wouldn't do the work required to grow her business.

We started working together and within four weeks Katherine wanted to quit. The sessions with her were painful, as she didn't want to do the work but wanted me to listen to how difficult her life was. It was as though I was her therapist, not her coach. She didn't do the work I gave her to do outside our sessions – work that would actually achieve her goal of having clients to serve. Working with her was draining my energy, because I'm not inspired to work with people who don't go all in. I tried to 'save' her, and she carried on for another four weeks, but ended up quitting. What's worse was that she logged a charge back via PayPal for the money she had paid – the money she was under contract to pay. She lacked integrity in many areas. It was a great lesson for me to listen to my inner wisdom.

Clients at this level aren't all like Katherine, of course – this was an extreme case. Some people in this bucket do want to learn, do want to do the work and are eager to expand, but they just take more time and energy from you because they're at the start line in their journey. You might love to work with these people and find it very rewarding, or you might not.

Perhaps you aren't inspired to work with people who fall into this category and prefer to work with people with a deeper understanding of your service area. Those people fall into the next bucket.

Level 6-10 clients

People who fall into this bucket tend to have experience in embracing challenges, and have been on a learning journey to deepen their awareness, skills and ability to transform. The gap you come in to help them fill is much smaller, but no less profound as they are able to take minimal guidance but understand and integrate it quickly.

They lead their outcomes and take responsibility for what they have and haven't achieved through your work together. They know that they co-create with you rather than waiting for you to lead them. Their mindset is that they know they will keep learning more and more, which will allow them to keep expanding and growing. They either want to work with you for an extended period or, after they stop working with you, they will quickly find the next mentor so they can keep expanding.

....

Level 6-10 clients invest in who they are BECOMING.

....

Have you worked with people like this? One of my clients, Jane, fits the description of investing in who she is becoming.

Like Katherine, Jane consumed several pieces of my content in one sitting and quickly booked a call with me. But she was very different from Katherine. Jane had an established business she had been running for over ten years, had an audience she wanted to better capitalise on, and wanted to work smarter rather than harder. On our call, Jane told me that her social media work was like throwing sand into the wind. She knew she was spamming her audience with a whole bunch of content that they weren't engaging with, and wanted to do the work to refine her message and build genuine connection. Working with Jane was like floating in a pool of water; it was calming and energising. In our sessions, I shared concepts and Jane would immediately understand them and make them her own. She took responsibility for her outcomes, did the work outside our sessions, and as a result the 6-10 level clients that she loves serving have continued to join and expand her monthly membership program.

Of course, people in this category don't come without challenges. Often they're fast-paced, big-picture thinkers, which means sometimes they go too quick and skirt over the important finer details. Your job as their coach or service provider is to navigate that with them to ensure they hear you properly, and don't miss lessons that are imperative to building a strong foundation and creating long-term success.

If you choose to focus on working with clients at this level, the benefit is that they're highly conscientious and take responsibility for their actions and results. You say one thing and, like a drop in the ocean, it ripples through them. They take it, apply it and get results. The problem with clients at this level is that there are fewer to choose from than there are in the 1-5 level bucket.

....

Whichever level of client you choose to focus on attracting and serving, the keys to success are knowing how to identify them and how to stand out from the noise and connect with them in a two-second world.

....

PROBLEMS, NOT PEOPLE

The classic customer avatar exercises you've done so far have not given you clarity on who to connect with on social media. These exercises don't work because you're designing details that don't have a real-world application and you're creating a character who doesn't exist. How can a pretend person find you and buy from you? How can you find a person who doesn't actually exist?

It's confusing at best, and at worst a complete waste of your time.

Part of the problem with those customer avatar exercises is they want you to outline your 'hero's journey', and list what book your avatar read or what they ate for breakfast. But when you go to find your people on social media, you can't work out if they're your 10% because your hero hasn't listed on their profile what they had for breakfast. (Unless you're on Instagram – then maybe you'll find a photo of their avocado on toast. Then you know with certainty they're your future client! And of course I'm being facetious here.) But even if you did know what they had for breakfast, you still don't know if they're a good fit for you because these ridiculous exercises won't tell you whether they're consciously aware that they have a problem and are actively seeking a solution. These exercises search for clients based solely on who they are as a person. And this is part of your problem, because your niche isn't always just a person – it's a problem that many different types of people have.

....

Your niche isn't always just a person – it's a problem that many different types of people have.

....

Your job is to get clear on both what the problems are that you can help people with, and all the different types of people who have those problems.

USE YOUR MUSE

One of the first things I do when I work with clients is get them to complete an exercise called 'Use Your Muse'. Whether they're looking to create a message that connects, craft content that converts, or get clarity on what their niche actually is, I remind them of the importance of not guessing or searching for information in their brain that might be half true. Instead, I get them to use a real person – namely, their muse.

....

Using your muse means picking a real person
you are going to reflect, speak from and speak
with when designing any business-related
communication material.

....

Using your muse means you select a real-life person – typically a client you've worked with and would love another ten clients just like them. Or you can select someone you had a sales call with who didn't convert to being a client, but who you would have loved to work with.

Once you've chosen your muse, you use that person's exact words and experiences in what you're creating.

When you do this, you get results. The communication material you create actually connects with many different types of people. You'll find more potential clients start reaching out to you, often saying things like, 'It's like you were reading my mind.' This is because you're now speaking from someone's real experience and using their words, not your words or the made-up words of a fictional character. Because it's real and one person in your target audience has experienced it, it resonates with many others in your target audience – because you're discussing and solving a problem experienced by many different types of people.

I'll give you an example of how this works.

Anthony was an experienced business owner, and had provided a done-for-you marketing service to brick-and-mortar businesses in his local area for over ten years. His business had grown predominantly via referrals and search engine optimisation, which had him ranked at the top of the first page of Google searches. But when he started his second business – an online business where he had to find and connect with a different market – he struggled. He was guessing when it came to choosing who to connect with, and using a fictional message that fell on deaf ears.

Anthony is a self-proclaimed 'bulldozer', and knows he has a habit of speaking *at* people even though he has the best of intentions. This bulldozer approach showed up in the way he was crafting his business message and content, and he was unsure of who to actually connect with on social media. This meant he wasn't seeing any conversion to clients from his efforts. But once he started applying the use your muse principle in how he engaged with potential clients online, he saw results immediately. Sales calls were booked, and clients were closed.

....

We use your muse in the context of identifying your niche so that you have complete clarity on who to connect with. You will then fill your school hall with your 10%, and when you do that your content connects and converts.

....

There are four simple steps to using your muse to identify your niche.

Step 1: Pick a person

Firstly, you want to pick a real person as your muse. As described earlier, choose a client you loved working with or someone you had a sales call with that you wished you could have converted. If you'd love ten more clients just like them, they'll be perfect as your muse. It might be that they have the same values as you, that they're committed to growing, that they take responsibility for doing the work and achieving the outcomes, or anything that is meaningful to you.

Got someone in mind? Great.

_____

_____

_____

Step 2: List their symptoms

Next, list all the symptoms this person told you they had *before* they started working with you. This is really important. You must list their symptoms, not their problems, and they must be symptoms they had *before* they started working with you.

Before your clients start working with you, they don't actually know what the root cause of their problem is. If they knew this, they wouldn't need you. What they *do* know is what their symptoms are. Their symptoms are all the things they say the problem is, even though these things are just by-products of the root cause of the problem. And the root cause is what you actually help them with.

For example, if I have a headache I will complain about a headache. But the headache is the symptom, not the problem. If I go to the doctor they will tell me I haven't drunk enough water and

I'm dehydrated, and that is the root cause of my problem. See the difference?

Maybe you're a relationship coach and you serve married couples to build a stronger relationship. The wife might tell you her husband doesn't listen, and the husband might tell you the wife doesn't want to have sex anymore. But both these things are symptoms, and you know that the root cause of their problem is that they have stopped communicating and each person expects the other to know what they're thinking.

....

You should list all your muse's symptoms in their words because this is what your target audience think their problem is, and you must communicate at their level of awareness, not yours.

....

_____

_____

_____

Step 3: Identify your school hall

Once you've listed all your muse's symptoms, using their words, list all the different types of people who have those symptoms and might be seeking a solution.

Using the example of the relationship coach, you might list men and women, but go deeper. What type of men end up with women who don't want to have sex with them because they're not an open communicator? Is it men who are in the finance industry because, typically, they're thinkers, not feelers, and are great with numbers but not with words? What type of women find themselves in marriages with men who don't meet their communication needs? Is it women who are nurses, who are often strong in their feminine energy and have a predisposition to expect to be saved by a man while also wanting to nurture and care for him?

Start with your muse, then look at other clients you've had. You want to accurately list all the different types of people who experience the symptoms your muse shared with you.

_____

_____

_____

Step 4: Eliminate!

Now you've got a list of symptoms and people who have those symptoms. But you won't be excited about serving every type of person on that list, so now it's time to do some elimination.

Take a look at the list and identify which people fall into the 1-5 level category and which fall into the 6-10 level category. Delete the types of people that you don't want to serve. What remains are the different types of people you *do* want to serve and who experience the symptoms you can help them with.

Using the example of the relationship coach, you might have a list that includes 'men who are financial planners'. So now, when you get on social media, you should be looking for men who list a career in the finance industry and have photos of their family on their profiles. You might even try to get an idea of how long they've been married. If it's more than five years, then you know that issues with communication and a lack of sex have probably started to surface. You can also check the content your target client is sharing for clues that his marriage is suffering. This is much more targeted than trying to work out if the picture of his avocado toast means he wants to have more sex with his wife.

_____

_____

_____

When you use this technique, you will add the right people to your school hall. Match this with dropping your I-centric messaging and replacing it with connected communication, as we discussed in Chapter 3, and you'll find that your content is converting prospects to clients.

....

That is the secret to having content that connects and converts to clients for you.

....

CLIENTS YOU LOVE AND MORE OF THEM

Once you know what level client you want to focus on, and you're clear on both the symptoms they have and the different types of people who have those symptoms, you can fill your school hall with people you can convert to clients through your content.

When you do this, you're on social media much less because your time is targeted; you know who to connect with and you're speaking with the right people who want help with what you offer.

It also means your content is connecting with these people because they're problem aware and solution seeking. This means potential clients will reach out to you after you post, and it won't just be Mum hitting the like button to show her support.

....

Now you're serving more people and serving people you love being with, and it means you have more time to do those things you enjoy in your business.

Sounds pretty good, right?

....

Lightbulb moment

Being in business and attracting clients can seem like a never-ending journey. If you're like most people, you don't want to market – you just want to have a waitlist full of clients and be focused on serving.

But if you're not consistently marketing your business, you're the equivalent of a billboard in the desert.

No doubt you've done heaps of work already on trying to understand your ideal client and where to find them. You wonder if you'll ever be 'done' with it. The truth is, you probably won't ever be done with understanding your ideal client, because they're real humans who, just like you, are constantly evolving. What you can do is keep expanding your understanding of them and how to better connect with them, so they choose you over your competitor. And most importantly, you should give yourself permission to fail a few times along the way.

If you aren't prepared to get it wrong, you're never going to get it right.

Thomas Edison made 10,000 attempts at creating the lightbulb. Isn't that inspiring? How many people do you know who would do something 10,000 times to perfect it? Would you? What's even more inspiring is that not only did Edison make 10,000 attempts to perfect the lightbulb, he said he didn't fail 9,999 times, but found 9,999 ways that didn't work.

Truly serving humanity and sharing your gift will require consistent and focused time, energy and action.

If you put focused energy into understanding your customers using the method laid out for you in this chapter, you'll improve your ability to create content that connects. And it's that connection that converts for you.

Key insights

- You're probably speaking to a lot of the wrong people – people who will never convert to clients (no wonder you're exhausted).

- It doesn't matter how connected your message is or how engaging your content is. If you haven't got the right people seeing it then it's never going to convert.

- Knowing the WHO, WHAT and WHERE of your 10% target audience that WILL convert is the key to consistent growth in your business.

- Classic avatar exercises are outdated and don't work. Trying to find "Avatar Amy" online, based on what she had for breakfast or what TV show she watches, is wasting your time because it's impossible and irrelevant.

- If you're not consistently marketing your business, you're the equivalent of a billboard in the desert.

CHAPTER 5

Relationships that relate

I f you build it, they will NOT come.

Right now, you have an expectation. You expect that if you build it, they will come. You expect that everyone will see what you see about how life-changing your service offering is, and that potential clients will just flow towards you and want to start working with you. You think that when you share content people will read it. You think they'll read or watch all the content you share, and that it will convert them because what you offer is so good!

Unfortunately, just building your offer and content is not enough to have a successful business that continues to grow, and we can see that truth in the statistics. The numbers don't lie. Twenty per cent of businesses fail in their first year, sixty per cent go bust within their first three years and ninety-six per cent close up before they reach ten years. Why? Apart from the fact that if you're not consistently marketing your business then you're the equivalent of a billboard in the desert, the other key factor is: RELATIONSHIPS.

Relationships are key to a successful and consistently growing business. If you and your competitor have a similar service or product, how does the consumer make their buying decision? It's largely based on how your brand and content make them feel.

The relationship you have with your clients and the way you make your audience feel is critical, and is largely why Apple has a fifty-six per cent market share in its competition with Android. When you purchase an Apple product, you're not just buying the operating system, you're buying into the community. Apple is known for being customer centric. The company creates a positive experience for the consumer from the moment you enter one of its stores. Its slogan, 'Think different', plays into its consumers' human need to be unique and have the best product in their possession. It's Apple's ability to connect and make the consumer feel that its products are an important part of their lives that has allowed the company to take a majority market share. Yes, the company built its product, but just building it wasn't enough. It's been Apple's ability to care for and connect with its audience that has made it the massive success that it is.

....

The relationship you create with your audience is why your audience will choose you over your competitor.

....

CAREFUL, CARELESS OR CARING?

You know you have a life-changing gift to share, so why aren't more people banging down your door and converting your offers?

You think you're being caring because you genuinely want to help your clients and are coming from a place of good intentions. But this is your I-centricity clouding your view and stopping you from seeing what's really going on. Your audience isn't hearing you because you're being either careful or careless.

One of my mentors taught me the concept of the Three Types of Relationships. The three types are *Careful*, *Careless* and *Caring*. Let's explore these in the context of communication and connection in your business.

In business and in life, you're creating and operating within one of the three types of relationships when you connect and communicate with others. These are not set; they are fluid and changing. Your mindset and the way you behave at any given moment determine which type of relationship you're creating with a person or group of people. Even though you may immediately think you're caring, you most likely are not.

Let's look at each type of relationship in more detail.

Careful

A careful relationship is one in which you care more about the other party than yourself, and is created when you minimise yourself in comparison with another person or group of people. You have put them above you, and think they have something you don't. You feel like you're walking on eggshells when you're around them and worry what they might think of you.

In this type of relationship you'll be overly giving of yourself, your time, your energy and your resources. Eventually you'll feel depleted and resentful towards the other party because there is imbalance between you.

This shows up in your business with clients and potential clients when:

- You criticise yourself for what you don't yet know or aren't doing.
- You let others dominate conversations.
- You hold back from making direct offers.
- You're scared of judgement and rejection.
- You wait for potential clients to reach out to you, and play a passive role in your client attraction.
- You undercharge for your service and then feel exhausted, because the revenue doesn't match the energy and time you give your clients.

If you're not getting conversion from your content and client attraction activities, you might be operating in a careful relationship, like my client Saalima was.

When I first started working with Saalima, she was frustrated and had very little energy left for her business. She was an expert-turned-coach with a background in social work and child protection. She had a plethora of qualifications as well as practical experience in non-traditional healing methods, which made her unique as a transformational coach. Like most coaches, though, Saalima didn't have consistent clients and was feeling drained by the clients she was serving.

We looked at her offer and I was shocked to learn that she was charging her clients just 2,000 dollars for twelve 1.5-hour sessions, as well as making herself available to them outside of sessions via email or Messenger. The time and energy Saalima was pouring into serving her clients did not match the price her clients were paying.

Saalima was also over-extending herself in the way she attracted these clients. She was spending hours every day on social media, but getting very little engagement and her activities weren't converting. She was tip-toeing around and creating conversations with potential clients, but was not forthright in making direct offers to them. The time and energy required to find and convert just one client was excessive. No wonder she was feeling disheartened about her business – she was being careful.

Can you relate?

Saalima and I worked on both her mindset and strategy. She now has an offer that she charges 18,000 dollars for, and she only spends one hour a day on social media to find, connect with and convert clients.

....

If you're walking on eggshells around your audience, holding back from sharing and connecting in fear of their response, you're being careful.

....

Careless

A careless relationship is one in which you care more about yourself than the other party, and is created when you maximise yourself in comparison with another person or group of people. You have put yourself above them and think you have something they don't. You have very little regard for what they think, and you may even be referred to as a 'bulldozer' in your approach to communicating and connecting with them. You'll believe you are 'right' and be focused on 'ticking boxes' when you connect with clients. This eventually leads to feeling ashamed, even though you may not publicly admit that.

This shows up in your business with clients and potential clients when:

- You talk about what *you* want rather than what *they* want (in your content, sales calls, client delivery). This is you projecting yourself onto your audience.
- You criticise clients for what they don't yet know or aren't doing (the very reason they need you!).
- You have I-centric content and messaging and salesy call-to-actions that aren't focused on the human, but *are* focused on the dollars.
- You expect potential clients to reach out to you, and play a passive-aggressive role in client attraction.
- You overcharge for your service and then get frustrated that more people don't see value in what you're offering.

If you're not getting conversion from your content and client attraction activities, you might be operating in a careless relationship – like Jamie.

Jamie came to me because she was tired of treating her audience like a booty call, and knew that she was only connecting with them when she wanted something. It wasn't going well for her. She had a one-of-a-kind product for real estate agents that could revolutionise the thing they hate doing the most and which takes up most of their time – prospecting. If Jamie could figure out how to meaningfully connect with her audience, she was sitting on a gold mine.

Do you feel the same way about what you have to offer?

Jamie and I worked on her connection, engagement and conversion strategy, as well as how she was creating messaging and content for her audience. We made sure there was less careless communication about what she wanted to give them, and more connected communication that accurately spoke to their experience and what they most cared about. As a result, Jamie's sales increased dramatically (she made twenty sales within the first seven days of a month, whereas she normally made no sales) and she had more time for her family. She isn't doing things in her business that don't convert, and has clear direction on what actions to take that give her the result she wants.

....

If you think your content and connection activities should prompt clients to come to you, and that you shouldn't have to reach out to them, you're probably being careless.

....

Caring

A caring relationship is one in which you equally care about what you want to give and what the other person or group wants to take. This type of relationship is built on the law of fair exchange, in which you present something of equal value to the other party in order to gain something from them. Both you and the other party are actively engaged in the relationship. This creates a strong and lasting foundation, which in turn creates trust – a by-product of fair exchange.

Zig Ziglar has shared that when you help others get what they want, you in turn get what you want. This is the basis of a connected and caring relationship.

This shows up in your business with clients and potential clients when:

- You have taken the time to understand what your audience wants, and you communicate your value in their values.
- You seek to understand what your audience doesn't yet know so you can help to educate them, as well as identify how you can keep strengthening your ability to convey your message to them.
- You are both proactive and responsive in your client attraction activities, and understand the importance of reaching out to potential customers as well as being engaged and attentive when they come to you. You both feel connected in the transaction.
- Your message is about what you have to offer and is expressed in a way that is most meaningful to them and what they want to take or have through your service or product.

- You are charging a fair price for what you offer.

It's unlikely that you'll ever constantly be in a state of caring in any relationship. It's more reasonable to expect that you'll oscillate between all three states. However, it is possible to be in a caring state for most of the time in a relationship.

Let's have a look at how one of my past clients addressed this issue.

Sheree had built a degree of success in her business and was sought after by organisations in her local area to speak to their staff about mental wellbeing. She was connected with me via a mutual business contact. Sheree wanted to set up an online coaching and mentoring business so she could create more freedom in her life and not be chained to doing in-person events. She had been in business for over ten years as a speaker and mentor, predominantly working in-person as a corporate consultant. When we first spoke, she thought all she needed to understand was how to set up an online learning platform and make sales from her courses.

What Sheree didn't realise was that as a speaker, she had become accustomed to speaking AT her audience rather than WITH them. Her dominant relationship style was to be careless. This wasn't translating well when it came to growing her online mentoring business, where she wanted to connect with and serve individuals rather than corporates, because she didn't have her reputation to rely on. Sheree had the best of intentions and didn't realise that she was often overwhelming her audience and over-delivering – she was being careless.

Sheree and I worked on how to structure her communication and how to give more to her audience by giving less, as well as how to understand what her audience were ready to hear and the words to use that would resonate best with them. When Sheree did this, she shifted her modus operandi to be caring and actually grew her speaking career. Her mentoring business also grew, because now both she and her audience were getting what they wanted – to be seen and heard.

....

You'll know if you've created a caring relationship in your business because you will be actively engaged in the pursuit of connection and conversion, but also have clients coming to you consistently from the communication you send out.

....

THE STING OF REJECTION

Putting yourself and your business out there requires a degree of vulnerability, and it's not always comfortable. You've likely had moments when you put yourself out there only to be left feeling rejected and wondering what's wrong with you.

....

In the context of the three types of relationships, you get rejected because you have acted from either a careful or careless place instead of with a caring intention.

....

Rejection is entangled with projection, so if you fear putting yourself out there it's because you projected instead of connected. As a result, you were rejected.

That sounds like an ambiguous tongue twister, so let's break it down and give you clarity on why more people are not signing up to your offers.

The word 'rejection' means 'throw away, to throw back'. Think about this for a moment. When you throw something away it's being pushed away from you. The direction of expression is outward. When you're being rejected by your target audience, they're pushing you outward and away from them, as Figure 1 shows.

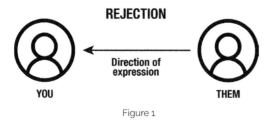

Figure 1

You can't throw something away without it first having come at you. This is how projection is entangled with rejection. For you to be rejected and pushed away, you first have to go forward – by projecting yourself.

The word 'projection' means 'thrust forward'. When you thrust your-self forward onto your target audience, they will throw you away and you will label it rejection, as in Figure 2.

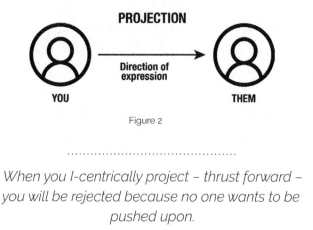

Figure 2

....

When you I-centrically project – thrust forward –
you will be rejected because no one wants to be
pushed upon.

....

You're only pushed away when you project, not when you connect.

FROM PROJECT TO CONNECT

The original meaning of 'connection' is 'the meeting of one means of travel with another, a circle of persons with whom one is brought into more or less intimate relations'.

The word 'circle' is important here, and tells you how to connect with your audience. Since a circle has no beginning or end, the direction of expression is fluid and continuous. In his essay on circles, Ralph Waldo Emerson spoke about how the centre of a circle is everywhere. This concept of circles and the centre being everywhere is useful for understanding the direction of expression to connect. Rather than I-centrically projecting yourself, you want to travel in a circular motion. This puts you in unity with your audience, where there is no beginning or end.

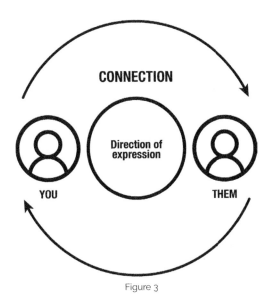

Figure 3

....

Circles have no beginning and no end, which means you are in constant connection with others when you caringly express yourself.

....

So how do you travel in unity with others and create connection? You ask quality questions.

QUALITY QUESTIONS CREATE QUALITY RELATIONSHIPS

The quality of your life and business is based on the quality of the questions you ask yourself and others. Quality questions bring forward truth, clarity and certainty for you and for the people you're in conversation with, either directly or indirectly. Quality questions present the answers that solve problems.

When it comes to your business, knowing the quality questions to ask will be the difference between growth and impact or staying stuck where you are.

The problem is that you think you're asking quality questions, but normally you aren't. Your I-centric nature causes you to ask questions from a place of what *you* want to know rather than what *they* want to talk about.

....

You ask questions from a place of what
you want to know rather than what
your customers want to talk about.

....

In the context of engaging with your target audience, you're probably not asking them questions at all, let alone quality questions.

You're likely doing what almost every service provider is doing. That is, either coaching or educating in your content and communication, which leaves the consumer with the impression that you've solved their problem and so they don't need to convert to a paying client.

When you share a message or communicate without asking a quality question, you're speaking AT your audience rather than WITH them. You might think you're starting a conversation but, unless you're asking a quality question, you're not. This speaking AT rather than

WITH people will show up in your content on social media, in emails you send out, and even in meetings and sales conversations. You have the best of intentions and want to show others what you know – that's your default I-centric position – but remember, others don't care what you know because they're I-centric too.

When you try to coach and educate others with your content, specifically your target audience in this context, you do yourself and your potential clients a disservice. This is because you give people a sense that they got the solution from your content and communication, even when you know they didn't. They can't possibly receive a transformation in its entirety without working with you.

This is the problem with always offering free content.

When you provide free coaching and education about your solution at the entry point of connection with potential clients, all you do is give them a dopamine hit. They *think* they got the solution, but you know that their problem can't be solved unless you do the deep work with them.

They consume your free coaching and education, and tell themselves they'll just go off and execute what they learned from you … except they don't. How many freebies have you downloaded from others and never used or even opened? A lot, right? It's the same for the people you're trying to serve. So, when you leave the impression that you coached them and educated them for free, you miss out on serving them. And they miss out on actually benefitting from your solution – because they think they already got it.

Before someone becomes your client, your only job is to leave them feeling seen. It's not to coach or educate them. It's to leave them feeling that you see and understand them, because when they feel seen, they naturally believe you have the solution.

When you're able to leave them feeling seen, you don't have to tell them to reach out to you for more information on what you have to offer. What you do is empower them to come to you so you can give them the critical skills they need for lifelong transformation.

The way to do this is by knowing what a quality question is, and asking it.

THE 3 ELEMENTS OF A QUALITY QUESTION

How many times have you opened up your social media platforms and seen a service provider ask the question: 'What's your biggest challenge with X?' Maybe you've done this, too? It's an attempt to conduct market research or find people who will tell you their challenges so you can identify specifically who to target as a potential client.

The problem with these types of questions is that you get little to no response. This is because you're asking people to look bad in public and feel ashamed, as well as trying to talk about their problems when you haven't earned that right – yet.

On the odd occasion that a question like that does get a lot of responses, you'll find that the responders are not the type of people you want to work with. If people are engaging in a public session about their problems, then they're more likely to be complainers than solution-seekers. The solution-seekers aren't responding publicly to 'biggest challenge' questions; they're off finding a solution.

Asking a quality question engages your target audience in a conversation in which you can learn a lot about them based on their response.

There are three elements to creating a quality question to ask your audience:

1. It must make THEM look good if they respond.
2. It must be EASY for them to answer – they must know the answer immediately. If they have to think about the answer for more than two seconds, they'll move on.
3. It must be what they WANT to talk about – not what you want to know.

All three elements must be present to create a quality question. If you want to know what someone's biggest problem is and identify who in your network has the problem you help solve, you *can* glean this information from them – but *not* by asking the 'biggest challenge' question.

For example, instead of asking your audience what their biggest challenge is, which makes them look bad and brings up shame, use the three elements just listed to craft a quality question. You'll get the answers you seek without upsetting your audience.

Here's an example of the difference between poor and quality questions:

Say I want my audience to talk about how they love creating content but run out of ideas. Rather than ask, 'Do you struggle to come up with ideas for content?', I ask 'Why would you choose to create content yourself over outsourcing to a VA?'

This brings forward the content creators. Only people who create content are going to answer that question, and by introducing the opposite approach – outsourcing to a virtual assistant – they naturally will tell me they love creating content BUT never seem to have enough ideas.

Framing the question in that way empowers THEM to answer, makes them look good and gets them talking about their problem. This allows you to make a meaningful connection. Your audience feels seen because they're the ones doing the talking, and this brings forward people you'd love to serve. So now both you and your audience get what you want. This is the difference between speaking *at* your audience and speaking *with* them.

Quality questions create quality conversations with quality people you want to serve.

Relationships build empires

In 1954, a girl was born into poverty in rural Mississippi. Her mother was an unmarried teenager. The girl was molested during her childhood and teenage years and became pregnant at the age of fourteen. Her son was born prematurely and died in infancy. After the death of her son, it would have been understandable if this girl had called defeat and given up on life or making an impact in the world. But instead, this young woman went on to land a job in radio while she was still in high school. By the age of nineteen she was a co-anchor for the local evening news. She became known for her emotion- and connection-centred approach with others, which boosted her career. She became a daytime talk show host, and eventually launched her own production company. She built her career based on her ability to interview others and ask quality questions that were not only engaging for those watching, but also left her guests feeling seen and heard.

This woman has since been inducted into the National Women's Hall of Fame, won many accolades – including eighteen Daytime Emmy Awards – and is the richest African-American woman in the world. She has been quoted as saying that she believes her success is largely a result of prioritising making a difference in the lives of others, and because she asks herself and others quality questions that build relationships.

That woman is Oprah Winfrey.

Key insights

- If you build it, they will NOT come. Just building a product or service will not be enough; you have to build relationships as well.

- Creating relationships with your audience is why your audience will choose you over your competitor.

- There are three types of relationships – careful, careless and caring. Two disconnect, one connects.

- As Zig Ziglar said, when you help others get what they want, you in turn get what you want. If you're getting rejected, then you haven't connected. You only get pushed away when you project yourself onto others.

- Knowing how to ask quality questions is how you create connected relationships, but often people ask questions from their I-centric nature. There are three elements to a quality question (see page 113).

What next?

Human connection is the source of light within you and around you.

As you've learned through reading these pages, when you go from I-centric communication to connected communication your relationships grow. Your business grows. You grow.

You feel more connected to yourself. This gives you greater confidence to show up in the world and create what you want.

You feel connected to others. You gain a deeper appreciation for all humans and a greater awareness of why they do what they do. You realise it's almost never a personal attack on you. It's simply their I-centricity.

You can take your newfound insights into your personal relationships.

You can take them to grow your business and share your message in a more connected way. As a result, more clients will be attracted to you, more clients will want to work with you, and you will have a bigger impact.

The key to this and anything we learn is: ACTION.

Don't let this book and what you've learned sit on the lonely shelves of your mind, collecting dust in the library of forgotten knowledge.

You must execute to integrate.

Execute to transform your I-centricity to connection.

That means using the exercises in this book to craft your new, connected message and then updating your communication materials to reflect it.

You must shift your approach to how you show up on social media. You need to do less speaking AT people with comments you think are helpful, and instead simply and meaningfully thank them for their contribution. They will feel seen, which in turn leaves you seen.

It means changing your content from 'I' statements to sharing what your audience wants to hear in a way that is about them.

When you execute what you've learned, you'll see the shift in how others respond to you. You'll see a new result in your business and life. You'll feel a deep sense of connection to yourself and others in a way you've never felt before.

Connection starts with you.

I'd love to hear from you – please email me and let me know what you took away from reading this book.

hello@opentograce.com.au

About the Author

In the pages before this one, you're going to remember the lost art of human connection and bring it forward in your business and life. I say 'remember' rather than 'learn', because you already have everything you need within you. This book is just about shining a light on what's currently hiding in the dark.

For this reason, I am not going to write an 'About the Author' in the third person. That is disconnecting, not connecting with you. We all know that the 'About' section was not written by a 'third person' – so let's stop pretending and start being authentic.

My love for human connection was sparked when, at the age of eleven, I was given the book *How to Win Friends and Influence People* by Dale Carnegie. It was then that my curiosity for understanding people and knowing how to connect with them began – and it hasn't stopped. I was acutely aware as a child, and well into my twenties, that I felt disconnected from myself and others and was often lonely. But the gift of that experience was being focused on understanding it and looking for ways to transform it, and ultimately to serve others by helping them do the same – because I knew it wasn't just me.

My mission is to directly serve one million people. I want to facilitate a pathway to take them back home to themselves through connection and understanding – of both themselves and others. Mentoring and teaching human connection and business growth is the vehicle that I do this through today.

I live in Sydney, Australia with my son, and when I'm not working on my mission you can find me practising yoga.

Website: https://www.opentograce.com.au/

Printed in Great Britain
by Amazon

24850017R00076